ALL EARTH IS CRAMMED WITH HEAVEN

ALL EARTH IS CRAMMED WITH HEAVEN

Daily Reflections for Mothers

MARY VAN BALEN HOLT

CHARIS

Servant Publications
Ann Arbor, Michigan

Charis Books is an imprint of Servant Publications especially designed
to serve Roman Catholics.

Scriptures quotations unless otherwise indicated are taken from THE
JERUSALEM BIBLE, © 1966 by Darton, Longman & Todd, Ltd.
and Doubleday, a division of Bantam Doubleday Dell Publishing
Group, Inc. Reprinted by permission. Verses marked KJV are from the
King James Version.

Published by Servant Publications
P.O. Box 8617
Ann Arbor, Michigan 48107

Cover design by Hile Illustration & Design, Ann Arbor, Michigan

96 97 98 99 00 10 9 8 7 6 5 4 3 2 1

Printed in the United States of America
ISBN 0-89283-920-1

Library of Congress Cataloging-In-Publication Data

Holt, Mary van Balen.
    All earth is crammed with heaven : daily reflections for mothers /
Mary van Balen Holt.
        p.   cm.
    Includes bibliographical references.
    ISBN 0-89283-920-1
    1. Mothers—Prayer-books and devotions—English.   2. Mother-
hood—Religious aspects—Christianity—Meditations.   3. Mothers—
United States—Anecdotes.   I. Title.
BV4529.H63   1996
248.8'431—dc20   95-50514
                                                                          CIP

DEDICATION

To the Mothers of my life:
Geneva Wheaton Harding
O'Tillie Rappel Van Balen
Geneva Harding Van Balen

And to all Mothers:
their far-reaching work
often done quietly,
hidden, unsung.

Contents

Acknowledgments

Introduction

Part 1: Family

The Tryout...19

When Life Clamors for Attention 21

Mother of the Bride 24

For Best, for Worst 26

Unbroken Circle of Love 28

"Hi, I'm Home!"...30

Traditions..32

Life with Mother 35

Piano Lessons 37

Reach Out and Touch... 39

Beginnings 41

Part 2: Friends

Patient Mercies...45

Threads of Friendship...48

A Gift of Tea 50

"Just-in-Time" Companions 52

The Contest 54

Transparency of Friendship 56

My Sister, My Friend..58

For Andrew...61

Befriending the Lonely...63

Helping Hands..65

On the Fringe 66

Part 3: Homefront

A Houseful of Gifts 71

Liturgy of the Hours 73

The Visit..75

Grace in the Kitchen...77

The One with the Vision...79

Our Place of Prayer 81

Rushin' and Runnin' 83

The Quality of Mercy 85

Time for Love 87

"Love Jesus Where You Are..." 89

Part 4: Good-Byes

The Measure of a Life 93

Endings and Beginnings..95

A Prayer of Tears..97

Presence 100

Divine Joy..102

The New Job..105

A Tool in the Artist's Hands 107

"Little Deaths"..110

Part 5: Wonder

The Measure of a Life 115

Moments of Awakening 117

What Feet Have Walked These Paths?...................119

"...and touch the face of God..." 121

A Renewed Spirit 123

Perception vs. Reality 125

God's Glory 127

Part 6: Waiting

Out of Control...131

The Line 133

A Visit to the ER..135

What Really Matters...137

Generations..139

Time for Prayer 141

Waiting Up 143

The Biopsy...145

The Flower...148

Part 7: On the Road

Making the Time to Talk 153

Living in the World 155

The Love That Binds Us...157

And a Little Child Shall Lead Them...159

"We're a Team"..161

Part 8: Nature

Desert Times..165

Monet's Sunrise 167

An October Morning..169

Focusing on the Present...171

Change on the Creek..173

The Hummingbird 175

The Flower Garden 176

Flood Relief 178

Part 9: Modern Sacramentals

A Constant Companion 183

On My Windowsill...185

Unexpected Sharing..187

Ordinary Things...189

The Boat..191

The Photograph..193

God in Our Souls...195

Notes...197

ACKNOWLEDGEMENTS

A book assumes final form through joined efforts of many people. I would like to thank those whose contributions helped turn my idea for this book into a reality.

The mothers who told their stories are too numerous to mention by name. Their faithfulness to the call of motherhood was an inspiration as well as a source of material. A special thank you to my sisters, Janet Distelzweig and Elizabeth Delphia and my parents, Joseph and Geneva Van Balen. Their prayers and support extend beyond this particular project in both time and scope.

My children, Joshua, Emily, and Kathryn, were most gracious about freeing their mother to work on this project. They willingly assumed more responsibility for household chores and running errands, and ate too many convenience food dinners without complaint. Their most important contribution, however, has always been being themselves and allowing me to include some of their stories in this book.

The greatest support came from my husband, Rick. Together we share the joys and challenges of parenting. While these reflections are told from my point of view, they have grown out of our combined faith, love, and commitment to each other and to our children.

Finally, I would like to thank all the people at Servant Publications, particularly, my editor, Heidi Hess. Her perceptive comments and enthusiasm for this book helped bring it to completion.

INTRODUCTION

☙

Earth's crammed with heaven, every common bush afire with
God: But only he who sees, takes off his shoes.[1]
Elizabeth Barrett Browning

This quote appeared at the end of a magazine article. It spoke to my heart and rests in a place of honor on my refrigerator door, right next to Thomas Merton's famous prayer that begins "My Lord God, I have no idea where I am going." Those two pieces of wisdom reign over my accumulation of school lunch menus, children's drawings, and family schedules. I read them and remember two things: I am not the only one who is unsure where life's commotion and struggle are taking me, and, God is as present in my kitchen as he was in the burning bush.

I like to think about earth being "crammed" with heaven. It reminds me of a suitcase stuffed until the hinges groan! My youngest packs that way to spend a night at Grandma and Grandpa's. She takes special things to show: a new dress, a favorite doll, dancing shoes. She wants to share her life with the people she loves.

God is like that. He fills creation with every good thing, every aspect of himself, because he wants to share his life with those he loves. This brimming creation could burst forth at any moment, showering us with new experiences or revelations of God.

But if earth is crammed with heaven and full of opportunities to encounter God, why don't we? Too often, God seems remote and inaccessible.

One reason can be found in our expectations, or more accurately, the lack of them. God is not expected to turn up in the laundry room or during late-night feedings. We don't expect to run into him in classrooms, department stores, or waiting rooms. A spiritual experience is not on the agenda for a day at the office as we sift through paperwork.

We expect to find God in churches, liturgical celebrations, and time set aside for prayer. Here is where we look diligently and are prepared for an encounter with the Holy One. Time spent in church or at special prayer is a modest part of our lives. If God reveals himself only at those times, chances for encounters are few. However God has crammed himself into all aspects of life. And when we *expect* to find the Holy One any place or any time, we will.

God did not choose an otherworldly manifestation to reveal himself to humanity. The Creator of the unfathomable cosmos clothed the greatest Mystery of all in the vulnerable, ordinary form of a human infant.

As years passed, God continued to reveal himself in ordinary events. Most people of Jesus' time did not see the whole reality in front of them. They saw the person, Jesus, but not the God who stood with them and walked their streets.

We are no different. We often do not perceive the sacredness in our midst. Instead, we see the ordinariness in which it is clothed. Jesus taught that whatever we do for one another we do for him. Still, we may not recognize the encounter with God when comforting a hurting child, supporting a struggling spouse, or helping a neighbor. Life abounds with opportunities to experience God through others. It is replete with moments of beauty, love, and joy that draw our hearts to the Maker. Still how difficult it is to recognize God in the midst of the busyness and mess of daily life!

We must practice. We must take time to reflect and be still, allowing God to reveal himself. The Spirit will lead. Jesus will make known the Father. Yet we cannot see if we do not look.

Jesus looked. He was an astute observer of life, as evidenced by the parables. He was reflective, and took time by himself to pray and be still. In events of his day, he discerned the voice of his Father.

God is speaking to us. The Sacred is infused into life. But we cannot hear if our world is filled with noise. We cannot see if we are too hurried to look.

When we do become aware of God in our lives, an appropriate response is to "take off our shoes." We acknowledge the Presence with a quiet moment, a prayer of thanks, a movement of the heart. It needn't be elaborate. As Browning says, "Only he who sees takes off his shoes." Our response is a sign of humility, a genuine offering of praise.

After Moses recognized God in the burning bush and removed his sandals, he was sent on a mission. God did not let him linger, sandals in hand, staring blissfully at the bush for the rest of his life. "Go. Free my people," God said. Reluctant though he was, Moses went.

The same is true for us. We cannot remain still, reflecting on the wonder of God-with-us. He has work for us: We must be his hands and feet, his heart in our world. We are mothers. We might be at home, in an office, or in a factory. We might be nursing the sick or teaching a child to read. We might be doing laundry, fixing meals, or cleaning house. Wherever we are and whatever we do, we are called to participate in the mission of Jesus.

To do that well, we must expect to find God in our everyday lives. Learning to see the sacred around us, we will live our ordinary lives knowing they are not so ordinary after all. God is truly with us, working through our hands and our hearts. God graces us with opportunities to encounter him not so we can rest quietly, forever enjoying the gift of the moment, but so we can be strengthened and empowered to do his work.

The Incarnation continues. What appears to be mundane is filled with things transcendent. Walking the earth we walk with our God, and life itself is a sacrament.

PART ONE

∾

FAMILY

The Creator of the universe revealed himself to us in a most vulnerable, ordinary form: a human being. From the moment of his birth he was drawing people to himself. The shepherds were first, followed by the townspeople. Children and adults alike smiled at Mary and Joseph as they proudly walked through the streets with their new baby. People caressed Jesus' cheek and made silly sounds, coaxing him to smile. They held out a finger hoping the infant would curl his tiny hand around it. They held him until he cried for his mother's familiar arms. God placed himself in the midst of his people, and they could not help but respond.

By his birth into a human family, God identified himself with us all. Every human being begins life in a family of one sort or another. We are daughters and sons, sisters and brothers, cousins, aunts, and uncles. Most of us grow into adulthood and become parents. We welcome new life. We complete the circle.

God's choice to enter our world through family honors that basic human community. It reminds us of the holy place family is meant to be. Jesus grew up with parents who loved and nurtured him. He must have toddled around under Mary's feet and in Joseph's shop. Later he helped them with their work. Together they prayed, studied, worshiped with the community, and served their neighbors. They laughed and cried. Spoke and sang. Celebrated and mourned together.

Mary and Joseph provided the home where Jesus grew in wisdom and grace. As he grew, so did they. How their prayer and understanding of God's plans for them must have changed over the years! How their faith was tested and strengthened!

Family is still called to be a sacred place. It is where we first experience God. Through its members he nurtures and cares for his people. He continues to reveal himself through those closest to us: our families.

This is not always easily realized. The family unit is under tremendous stress. Pulled in a myriad of directions, its members strain to live in a way that allows the home to be a place of grace and support.

In the midst of this struggle, God is there. In our failures as well as successes, he speaks to us through one another, children and parents alike. He blessed the family when he chose it as his place to be for most of his life on earth. He blesses our families. Our challenge is to recognize his presence in the midst of what is most familiar.

THE TRYOUT

*I saw that he is to us everything which is good and
comforting for our help. He is our clothing, for he is
that love which wraps and enfolds us, embraces us
and guides us, surrounds us for his love, which
is so tender that he may never desert us.*[1]
Julian of Norwich

There we were, my two daughters and I, sitting on folding
chairs hastily set up around a piano and collapsed risers in
the high school choir room. The drama club needed twelve
younger students for parts in the musical. We were waiting for
tryouts along with seventy other hopeful children and their parents.

I watched children practicing their songs and creating motions
to go with them. When one group returned from the auditorium,
others rushed over for information: "What did you have to
do?" "You had to act like a **dog**?" I saw the happy faces of those
asked to stay for further auditioning and the brave faces of others
as they hurried to leave.

While one of my daughters is a veteran of these tryouts, this
was a first for the youngest. The night before auditions she could
not sleep. "What will I do if I don't get a part?" she worried. "I
don't know if I want to get a part. I mean, if I'm this nervous
about tryouts, what would I do if I got one?"

I hugged her. "You don't have to try out," I said. "You're too
tired now to decide. I love you no matter what you do." Finally,
she slept.

In the choir room, I watched her struggle with her feelings

and the long wait. She stood up when her name was called, and joined the group going to the auditorium. She didn't look back. She would try out, even if it meant acting like a dog or a piece of sizzling bacon. Even if it meant getting a part.

~

Sometimes I am afraid to try, to risk looking silly, or to fail. Like my daughter, I am sometimes afraid of success. It brings responsibilities and requires commitment. I am filled with a mother's love as I watch her go. I want to nurture her, to protect her, and yet, I know I need to let her grow.

God, go with her. She walks into the unknown with her child's faith in you, in me, in herself. Be with me as I walk into my life's unknowns. Help me believe, with Julian of Norwich, that you love us with a mother's love and that "...all shall be well, and all shall be well, and all manner of things shall be well."

WHEN LIFE CLAMORS
FOR ATTENTION

∾

*The world is not a vacuum. Either we make it an altar
for God, or it is invaded by demons.²*
Abraham Heschel

It was a minor inconvenience. I would have to drive my husband's small car instead of the minivan I use to run the children around town. Why did I rankle so? I was ready to walk out the door to a speaking engagement and the rest of the family was heading for showers and then church when suddenly, no water.

We had been gambling with the hot water tank for months. It needed work, but never as urgently as some other household repair. We ignored it and tore up the bedroom carpet instead. We decided a family weekend away was more critical. The car's oil needed to be changed. The water heater waited and leaked a little more.

Why this Sunday did it finally decide to clamor loud enough to demand attention?

"You'll have to take my car," Rick said. "I'll need the van to bring home a new tank."

I knew he was right. Still, I mumbled and complained while putting on my coat and gathering my books.

"I hate your car. It's so low, my sore knee hurts just getting in! And that stupid mat under the clutch," I muttered. "I have to pull it back just to start the car."

As I grumbled complaints, my dark mood deepened. Rick carried out the box of books. I took the briefcase. We loaded them onto the back seat.

"Bye! Good luck!" He smiled and waved.

"Bye. See you later." I replied. My smile was weak. I felt guilty and foolish. Driving up the freeway, I replayed the incident in my mind. What if, after registering my disappointment, I had smiled instead of strewing complaints in my wake? What if I had recognized that my husband's plans had also been abruptly changed? He wasn't complaining. What if I had told him I appreciated his staying home to make repairs while I went off for an enjoyable afternoon engagement? I imagined we would have parted feeling closer and with a sense of common purpose. We would be busy at different tasks. Each would appreciate the role the other was playing.

Why had I sabotaged the opportunity? Instead of building up our relationship, I had chipped a bit of it away.

~

As a teen I was cautioned about playing with Ouija boards. "Evil spirits are in the world," the nuns had said. "You don't want to open the door for them, not even a crack." I thought they were overreacting. Growing older has enabled me to see the wisdom in their warnings. But the danger is more immediate and insidious than an Ouija board.

Evil does exist. Like dust or sand or water, it will enter the smallest crack and begin to change what lies within. Like dust, the presence of evil is often difficult to see at first. When do the dust particles land and coat the end table or computer? You don't see them until they collect into a thick layer. A wipe with a rag, and they're gone.

A relationship isn't as easy to restore. Bit by bit, we let opportunities to strengthen it turn into moments of erosion. Such small bits are chipped away that we rarely notice them, until one day we become aware of feeling distant, detached, or resentful.

Evil is at work in the world. My own self-pity was the crack that let it into our Sunday morning; once it was there, allowing my sense of disappointment to grow was easy. Self-pity feels good for awhile, and it is easier than reaching out to the other.

Lord, help me recognize the Evil One chipping away at the relationship between my husband and me. Help me remember that you are part of our marriage covenant. You have already overcome the world. Lend me your strength to shut the door, to fill the cracks that craze my life.

Mother of the Bride

Christ has no body now on earth but yours, no hands but yours, no feet but yours; yours are the eyes through which Christ's compassion looks out at the world, yours are the feet with which he is to go about doing good, and yours are the hands with which he is to bless us now.[3]
Teresa of Avila

With five daughters and two sons she has been the "mother of the bride" twice before. But this wedding will be different.

"With a large family, I didn't expect everything to be, well, *usual*," she says. "But I never expected this."

Her daughter, Janice, is marrying a widower with two children. He is black. Janice is not.

"We love him," the mother muses. "At first we didn't know what to say. Now we talk late into the night. We laugh and play cards. He's one of the family. The children love him. When they're wrestling around on the floor, David's in the middle of it. The rest of us just smile and step around them all! His children are delightful. But..."

Her voice trails off. Her eyes gaze at some distant point, searching for understanding and wisdom. She looks for a long time.

"Who will affirm their marriage?" she finally asks. "We needed a while to open our hearts to David and Janice and their commitment to each other. If we had trouble, who in this world will welcome them?"

She stares into the distance again. This time seeing pain, hurt, and frustration for the future family.

In the quiet, I remember a high school friend's interracial wedding in the late sixties. She was the captain of the cheerleading squad; he was the football star. Their romance and marriage had anguished her family and angered some of our classmates. That was the sixties. This is the nineties. Amazingly, the question still remains: Who will welcome them?

~

Lord, we try to teach our children to love and accept as you do. But when they do, they challenge our own ability to do the same. We are older. We know more of the mean-spiritedness loose in the world. We have seen the problems and the tragedies. Life is not fair. Good hearts and sincerity are no protection. And yet, it is your kingdom that our children are trying to build, just like you asked. Maybe our older eyes don't see as well as we imagine. You never promised an easy path. "Choose me," you said, "and I will be with you."

Help us trust your presence in those who choose you. They will be the ones to welcome our children. In their arms, David and Janice will find your support. You hold us, as you promised, with the arms and hearts of your people.

FOR BEST, FOR WORST

*I will love thee even as myself. I will keep faith and loyalty to
thee, and in thy necessities aid, and comfort thee...*[4]
Byzantine Rite of Betrothal

She walked along the beach with her children. The stiff, salty
breeze made her hair fly up, like a mane around her face.
Drinking in the early afternoon air, she felt every part of her body
tingling and alive. The morning had been a refreshing change.

"Mom! Look at this!" Her son, far ahead of her and the two
younger boys, returned with a sea treasure in his hand.

"A hermit crab!" he panted. "Look!"

His two brothers squatted and watched as the little creature
picked its way in front of them, leaving tiny, wedge-shaped tracks
in the hard sand.

"Isn't he great, Mom? Mom?"

She was lost in thought, gazing at the horizon. The morning
had been peaceful. Just she and the three boys. They had run
with abandon into the surf for a morning swim and then spent
hours playing in waves and tidepools. Now the morning was
gone. The boys were hungry. So was she. They needed to get out
of the sun.

"Get your sandals and buckets. It's time to head back for
lunch," she said, feigning a nonchalance that belied the fear
churning her stomach. She steeled herself for their return to the
beach house.

Would her husband meet them angrily at the door, upset by
their long absence? Would his rage, fueled by drink, pour over
them as they walked in, or would he be quiet and sullen? She

played out the scenes in her mind. He might be drunk, asleep on the bed. She hoped so.

"It didn't start out like this," she thought as they walked back toward the boardwalk. "Not in the early years. A drink or two a day, to unwind. That's what he said."

She held the youngest one's hand tightly. His small, soft fingers were at once reassuring and accusing. She would have to do something. This was no way for young boys to grow up. This was no life. Stepping on a sharp piece of shell protruding from the sand, she winced. Tears came to her eyes, and she let them come. Quietly they ran down her face, mingled with tears that sprang from another, deeper hurt.

~

For better or worse. Why do those words slip so easily through the lips of couples on their wedding day? No one thinks the "worse" will happen to them. But it does. For some the "worse" is more serious than for others. But all couples have times that stretch their faith and commitment to the breaking point. Lord, strengthen us as we try to remain faithful to our covenant, to our spouses, to ourselves. You have called us to bring your healing love to one another. Sometimes that requires confrontation and pulling back. Guide us so the actions we take are chosen out of love and desire to help each other grow closer to you.

UNBROKEN CIRCLE
OF LOVE

∾

*One time after I had given a talk to a large library- association
annual meeting, one of the librarians asked me "What do you
think you and Hugh do that is best for your children?"
And I answered off the top of my head, "We love each other."*[5]
Madeleine L'Engle

Streamers and balloons decorated the hall. Occasionally a child
ran by, batting an errant balloon. I sat at the white, cloth-
covered table and surveyed the room. The church basement had
been transformed into a fitting place to celebrate my parents' fifti-
eth wedding anniversary.

The most striking feature of the room, however, was not the
decorations, but the people who filled it: family and friends from
eight months to eighty years of age.

I was glad to see my father's brothers. How many weddings
had they celebrated together? Dancing with my uncles had been a
highlight of family weddings for me as a child. I smiled and
watched them line up for a picture. Still clowning, still tall and
straight and handsome.

A baby's hungry cry rose above the conversation and music. It
was Jenny's son. Over the years Jenny's family and ours had
become very close. Her parents, Pat and John, had become our
neighbors before Jenny was born. Far from home, they looked to
my parents for support as they raised their growing family. When
Jenny's twin brothers arrived, one of them had a physical problem that required surgery and special care. Mom would some-

times watch the young twins, giving Pat and John an occasional night out. Now Pat and John live in Texas, and were unable to come to the celebration. But Jenny was there.

Small groups clustered around the room. There were neighbors who had gone through the school years together. They carpooled, organized Girl Scouts, and worked bingo. My father's co-workers had come. I hadn't seen them since I was a young girl. Sitting two rows away were Mr. Whalen and his wife. I still call him "the insurance man," but years of long talks around my folks' table made him one of their dearest friends.

The people were the true ornament of the room: old friends who had become "family," so closely had their lives become entwined with ours; new friends who added fresh sparkle to the festivities; aunts, uncles, and cousins; children of children my parents had watched grow. "Who's that?" my daughter asked, nodding toward a white-haired couple laughing with my parents. "That's Mr. and Mrs. Stuckey. She always helped Grandma when we had big family celebrations...."

~

Lord, it is good for the younger generation to see marriage this way: real people, real lives with day-to-day struggles and triumphs. Children, teens dating, the newly married, Jenny with her infant son: our lives have all been touched by the beauty and grace of these older couples' lifetime commitments. Your love that is present in them speaks a message our world needs to hear: Marriage is good. It is holy, a gift to be treasured. It is worth all the work and sacrifice needed to keep it vital. Marriage is something to celebrate!

"HI, I'M HOME!"

~

"I'm tired of coming home to notes instead of people."
Kathryn Holt

"I'm home!" The door slammed behind me. I looked at the
kitchen clock before walking into the dining room. It was
already six. The house was quiet.

"I'm home," I repeated.

"Hi, Mom," said a voice from behind a bedroom door.

"I'm up here," said another from the room across the hall.
Two out of three. I was mentally checking them off: children
safely home before their mom. I glanced around. The chores out-
lined for them on my morning note had been done. Footsteps on
the stairs announced that the third and youngest child, Kathryn,
was home, too.

I sank into our favorite living room rocker, waiting for the
wonderful warm moments when she would crawl into my lap and
tell me about her day.

She didn't. She stood in front of me, looking straight into my
heart with her sad green eyes.

"I'm tired of coming home to notes instead of people," she
declared. "How long does this thing at work last?"

I pulled her onto my lap and pressed her close to me. Burying
my nose in her sweet hair, I sighed and kissed her.

"I'm sorry, Hon. Every day I think I'll get home early, and
every day I have so much to do I end up working late."

"I hate notes. 'Cookies on the counter. K, don't forget to
practice piano. J, please put the trash can back into the garage...'"

Her voice trailed off. My stomach felt sick. This wasn't how I had imagined life with a part-time job. The overstuffed rocker moved slowly back and forth as we sought solace in the ancient rhythm. Each lost in our own thoughts, we sat together. Through the window we watched evening come. We were two thieves, stealing moments from a lifestyle that had none to spare.

~

Not many years ago, I spent my days at home cooking and doing laundry. Or so it seemed, anyway. People told me they were the best days, and to enjoy them. I did, most of the time. But sometimes while I was trying to take a moment for myself by hiding out in the bathroom, I imagined what it would be like to work somewhere else. On those days almost any job out of the house sounded good. After all I had a college degree and had worked before we were married and had children.

Lord, now I stand in line at the grocery store, holding frozen pizza in my hand, and wondering why I'm working somewhere besides home. I look at the other working mothers in line. Some look smart in their business attire. Some just look worn out. How can we do it, Lord? I imagine they are all doing better than I. Maybe I'll learn how to juggle family and job. I'm not sure I want to. In the meantime, help my family understand. I love them. I'm doing my best.

TRADITIONS

❦

And when the day came for them to be purified as
laid down by the Law of Moses, they took him up to
Jerusalem to present him to the Lord, observing
what stands written in the Law of the Lord.
Luke 2:22-23

October. The month of our annual family weekend away had finally arrived. For years we have rented a rustic cabin tucked into the Hocking Hills of southern Ohio and left the busy world behind. For three days, no telephones or television. We have time to play games, read, and hike. We have time to be family.

But as the weekend approached, we were discouraged. An early onset of bronchitis coupled with the flu had had me out of circulation for a month. As someone wryly observed, it wasn't like I was dead, but almost. The children got up, fixed their breakfasts, packed lunches, and got themselves onto the bus. Cloistered in my bedroom listening, I was too worn out to help.

The trip to the woods seemed out of the question. Reservations had been made, but we were prepared to cancel. Or so we thought.

The weekend dawned with snow on the ground. Snow! We love the woods flocked with early snow. Suddenly, everyone wanted to go. Sleeping there would be impossible for me, but the cabin is close to our home. I could at least go for a day.

Sleeping bags, games, and books were thrown into cars. Logs, boots and extra clothes were next. One car, filled with people and gear, left for the cabin. I followed, stopping by the store for food we didn't have on hand.

My heart pumped faster as I drove down the township roads,

which hug the creek bed and wind through the valley. All around me were rusty hills etched with snowy-branched trees. The frosty powder clung to windward sides of rocks and cornstalks. I rounded the last bend and saw chalky smoke rising into the darkness from the cabin's stone chimney.

I got out of the car and drank deeply of the star-splattered night. Inside, the no-match fire (started with flint and steel by our son) was blazing away. Gear lay in heaps on the ping-pong table. Water for tea was boiling in a dented aluminum pot on the old gas stove. The familiarity of the place greeted me and wrapped me up like a favorite, old blanket. Thoughts of work, school, and deadlines fell away.

We made a few trips to the car to bring in the last supplies. Before long we were gathered around the kitchen table playing a game and washing down snacks with cider. The ritual family time had begun.

~

Traditions give a framework, a stability to our lives. Without realizing it, we use them to mark time, to regain perspective, to remember who we are. Jesus, your family knew the importance of traditions. They presented you at the temple. They observed Sabbath rituals and prayers. You attended friends' weddings and funerals. Keeping traditions is work. Sometimes fatigue or illness weigh me down. Even bedtime prayers can seem too much when I am collapsed on the couch after a long day. I'm tempted to let the rituals go unobserved. "It doesn't matter," I say to myself. But I know better.

It matters because our traditions have helped define who we are, what we believe, and where we belong. Lord, help me persevere when I am weary. When I feel too tired to make a special birthday dinner, or make the vegetable soup we "always have," help me remember your mother, preparing the Sabbath meal. (Did you remember them on Sabbath nights, when you were out on the road with your disciples?) Help me think of you, young and at prayer around your family's table, when the trappings of our rituals seem overwhelming. Help me remember, Jesus, because it matters.

LIFE WITH MOTHER

∿

Like a son comforted by his mother
will I comfort you.
Isaiah 66:13

We sit there, my mother and I, across a kitchen table full of nicks and scratches put there years ago by my brothers and sisters and me. The talk is about her friends, my children, and who will bring what to Thanksgiving dinner at the farm.

My mind wanders. I think of my mother as a young wife and mother of five. She steadied my hand as I learned to maneuver cereal from bowl to mouth. Now I look at her fine, white hair, her thickly veined hands, and wonder that this is the same woman. My stomach knots up and a rush of sadness sweeps over me. I want her back, her hair more pepper than salt, her skin smooth and young.

She is tired from planning and preparations for the big dinner. Her hand quivers and tea spills on the table.

"I'll get it, Mom."

I slide out of the chair and hurry to the sink for the dish cloth. I hate to watch her getting old. Or thinking of life without her.

∼

My young mother has grown through the middle years and into old age. One day she will be with you, Lord. Somewhere, but not here. Letting go of my mother, and trusting her to you is not always gracefully done. Sometimes I want to grab time and turn it back, or at least hold it still.

I cannot imagine life without her. Yet, sometimes I lack patience to deal with the effects advancing years have had on her. Help me see past the aging body to the spirit that remains vibrant and eager to be a part of my life. Lord, help us both embrace this season of life with trust as well as love.

Piano Lessons

*And David danced whirling round before
Yahweh with all his might...*
2 Samuel 6:13

Fresh from sleep, our five-year-old daughter sat on the floor. The hand-me-down flannel nightgown was gathered around her feet. Tossing her long, blonde hair from her eyes, she bent intently over the keyboard, searching for notes.

I recognized the familiar melody: "The farmer in the dell. The farmer in the dell." Those notes came quickly. They had been mastered the night before. What came next was more difficult.

"Hi ho the derry..."

She tried again.

"Hi, ho the derry-o, the..."

She shook her head. "Nope," she whispered to herself, beginning again.

After several experimental starts and corrections, she succeeded. The whole tune spilled out of the keyboard and hung in the air. She played it again to make sure the song was hers to command and not just a lucky accident.

It was hers! She looked up, eyes sparkling. "I did it! I did it!" she cried to no one in particular. She began to dance around the keyboard. The nightgown billowed as she twirled and skipped through the room. She hummed the song in her heart, swinging her arms in time to her own music. She caught my eye. Smiling, she crossed the room and threw her arms around me in a triumphant hug.

"I can do it, Mom! I can do it!"

~

I am humbled in the presence of such genuine celebration. Her dance was pure joy. It was prayer, not performance. She could respond immediately and naturally to the wonder of music and the ability to produce it with a touch of her fingers.

Lord, it is your creation that touched her heart, and she could respond, like David, with dance. I am often too self-conscious to express the joy and praise I feel in my heart. I worry about how I will look or what I will sound like, and the prayer becomes lost.

Thank you for the gift of my children. They are not an extension of myself, but a reflection of you that brightens the world. Their uninhibited response to the joy you have put into creation refreshes my spirit. Mary must have known such moments with Jesus.

Reach Out and Touch

~

*Love alone is capable of uniting living beings in such
a way as to complete and fulfill them, for it alone takes
them and joins them by what is deepest in themselves.*[6]
Pierre Teilhard de Chardin

After giving Mary communion, I sat with her and her husband, Ralph, for our weekly visit. She brought me up to
date on her grandson's new life in the navy.

"Chris called the other day." Mary's eyes sparkled. "From
Hong Kong! The phone rang and I picked it up. I heard 'Hi,
Grandma,' just like he was across the room. Didn't he, Ralph?"

"Eee-yep," he nodded.

She shook her head. "He loves it, just **loves** it. It's good to
hear so much enthusiasm in his voice. He was always so quiet,
you know. He's just found his place. The navy. He's still trying to
get into the Seals."

She sat properly in her chair, her eyes smiling. Her hands
played with the edge of her sweater and opened and closed in her
lap. She pointed to his picture on the book shelf. I picked it up
and admired it.

"He's not one to write much. We always told him, 'Now
Chris, you know you can call us anytime.' But imagine, from
Hong Kong!"

She paused.

"It's nice to know he wants to keep in touch."

~

Lord, the love you give us to share with our children and their children stays with them forever. They can draw on it when they are in need, close at hand or far away.

Sometimes I am tempted to give my children things, or what is the current passion: opportunities, at the expense of time together. Help me to remember that what lasts is love. Long after toys or clothes or books are forgotten on some dusty shelf or in some dark closet, the relationship we have will remain. The love we share will bring us together, even if we are halfway around the world.

BEGINNINGS

Every child comes with the message that
God is not yet discouraged of man.[7]
Rabindranath Tagore

I took my daughters to Ellen's house for a haircut. They were excited to see the new baby. Ellen's two older girls raced through the house to meet us at the door.

"We have a baby! Wanna see it?"

Of course we did. My daughters examined Allison as she squirmed in her plastic carrier. She started to cry and I offered to hold her while Ellen got busy on the girls' hair.

Once the baby was in my arms, I began the gentle swaying motion all mothers know. Allison and I walked through the house. Her head bobbed to the side and I slid my hand quickly to cradle it. She whimpered. Her head pressed into my shoulder and lolled backwards. I was out of practice. Shifting her position, I tried ones that had quieted my children: the hanging-over-your-arm hold, where the baby's stomach rests on your arm and her arms and legs dangle freely; the face-out-and-look-around hold; the over-the-shoulder hold. After some jostling, swaying, and quiet humming, Allison fell asleep.

I sat on the couch and studied her face. Her skin felt like velvet. Her breath was sweet. Her tiny fingers curled around anything they touched. Even asleep, she was exploring her new world, drawing in everything around her, learning to live her gift of life.

Allison stirred, stretched her hand, and grabbed my cracked, wrinkled finger with her smooth, plump one. I smiled. As middle-aged as I am, I didn't feel so far from beginnings.

~

Lord, holding this baby makes me aware of the newness of life. Not just for infants, but for all of us. Every day is a chance for new beginnings. I met a pilot who had been in an accident and had lost both legs. He flew again. He went to college at forty and became an engineer. He wrote a book when he was in his seventies.

Sometimes when choices I have made seem to set an unalterable course, I forget that life begins fresh every day. Unlike Allison who is experiencing life at every moment, I just go through the motions. Routine and fast pace dull my perceptions. One middle-age affliction is thinking the choices have already been made. Many have. Not all.

The pilot couldn't undo his choice to fly the day of his accident. His life was changed forever. But he could choose what he would do next. He depended on you, Lord. He drank in opportunities and made choices that affected his life significantly. Lord, you are constantly inviting me to join you in creating life, in deepening my own life in you. Help me be open to the possibilities for new beginnings.

PART TWO

FRIENDS

Perhaps because hospitality was one of my parents' greatest gifts, I love to imagine Mary, Martha, and Lazarus welcoming Jesus into their home when he dropped by. What a pleasure the visit must have been! His presence meant good conversation, the kind that engages spirit as well as intellect. They might have laughed about something funny Jesus saw as he traveled, or the antics of a young boy in the market. Despite Martha's preoccupation with domestic chores, I'm sure Jesus was eagerly received, no matter what the house looked like.

I think of times when unexpected visits have surprised and delighted me. Clutter is shifted to one end of the table. We take time drinking not only tea and coffee, but each other's company as well.

Sometimes I call a friend when my spirit or body needs support: a child is struggling, bronchitis strikes, a relationship is strained. And friends come. They sit at the end of my bed or a telephone line and listen.

Friends bring wisdom, memories, and more questions. They laugh and cry at our predicaments.

Friends are responsible for each other. My friend Eileen can always be counted on to deliver her steaming pot of homemade chicken soup, fragrant with tomato, rice, potato, and onion. The food deliveries go both ways. Each one of us has gifts to offer as well as needs to be filled.

Because openness creates vulnerability, friends can also be a source of pain, separation, loss, and misunderstanding. Mary, Martha, Lazarus, and Jesus knew that side of friendship as well. They shared concern for Jesus' work. Lazarus' illness and death made his sisters wonder why Jesus had not been there to cure him. Lazarus' death moved Jesus to weep, and his own suffering and death left his friends anguished.

Anyone who is a friend, anyone who has a friend, knows the relationship intensifies life's experiences and emotions. Friendship is a blessing. It is a gift. At a time when schedules and technologies can work against establishing and maintaining such relationships, friendships are worth the effort they require.

St. Thomas Aquinas said that nothing on earth is more prized than true friendship. Jesus chose to be part of a web of friends while he walked the earth and shared our human existence. He continues to desire true friendship with each one of us. Our own friends are a reflection of that desire.

PATIENT MERCIES

∾

....then he happened to notice a poverty-stricken
widow putting in two small coins, and he said,
"I tell you truly, this poor widow has put in more
than any of them; for these have all contributed
money they had over, but she from the little she
had has put in all she had to live on.
Luke 21:2-3

The phone rang. Mary grabbed her cane and carefully walked into the living room.

"Hello?"

"Hello, Mary? This is Clare."

"Yes! I've been thinking you'd call." Mary sat down and rested her cane against the chair. Shifting the phone to her right hand, she strained to hear the voice at the other end, asking "how are you, Mary?"

"Well, this has been a pretty good week. I'm still unsteady on my feet, but at eighty-two what can you expect?" Mary laughed a little at her own predicament. Her sense of balance had deteriorated. She rarely trusted herself to go outside. Without her husband's steady arm, she'd never ventured beyond the house. Clare's call brightened the day. Usually it meant she was coming to bring communion and visit. How Mary had grown to love the younger woman. Had three years really passed since they were paired by the parish homebound committee? She blessed the day. "Yes, I'm a little wobbly, but ready for a visit!"

She thought of the time Clare spent with them. She rarely hurried in and out. After communion and prayer she stayed and talked. Sometimes Ralph would call out for fish sandwiches and they'd have lunch. Clare rarely refused a cold drink or a sandwich. Mary was glad she didn't. There was little else she could do to return Clare's kindness.

"I wanted to talk with you about that, Mary. I put off coming until Friday because I thought I could get through all this work on my desk by then. But then Emily got sick and I'm so far behind..."

Mary jumped in. "Clare, let's just forget it this week. I appreciate all the time you spend here."

"Well, I was thinking I could come later this evening."

"Now, Clare, you just forget about it. You have to take care of your family first. We'll just let it go and I'll see you next week."

Mary was thinking. She'd need to put the homemade pimiento cheese back into the refrigerator. She had set it out to soften. Clare liked it so. "Are you sure, Mary? I could be out there by 4:30."

"No, you just stay put. You're a busy woman. Just get done what you've got to do and don't give it a thought." Mary knew Ralph would be disappointed. He had finished the jigsaw puzzle Clare commented on last week. He wanted her to see it before taking it apart.

"Well, if you're sure you don't mind. I appreciate it, Mary. This desk is swamped. I'll miss you, though. That goes for Ralph, too. I'll call Monday or Tuesday."

"That will be fine. Now you go and get to work. I'll see you soon."

Mary carefully placed the receiver back and reached for her cane. Slowly easing out of the chair, she made her way into the kitchen and put the pimiento cheese back into the refrigerator.

~

Does Mary know the gift she has given? She has relieved a little pressure from a "pressure cooker week." Clare knows. Humbled before such selflessness, she knows the greater loss is her own.

Lord, you give us time to become who we are meant to be. You wait. Like the older friend, you are present for us when we are ready. There is no hurry. Love is always receiving and holding, wherever we are on our journey. In a world that runs on deadlines, clocks, and schedules, your patience is mercy.

THREADS OF FRIENDSHIP

*To you, I am nothing more than a fox like a
hundred thousand other foxes. But if you tame
me, then we should need each other. To me,
you will be unique in all the world. To you,
I shall be unique in all the world..."¹*
Antoine de Saint-Exupéry

After a busy day running errands, I rushed home to pick up
children at school. I pulled into the driveway and turned the
key. The engine stopped, but I couldn't make myself move. I sat,
wishing the "Radio Reader" was still on the air to read me a
chapter or two while I melded with the seat.

Opening the car door, I slowly walked up the side steps. A box
addressed to me from Linda was propping open the screen door.
A friend from college days, Linda is now a doctor on the west
coast. We don't see one another, but we write and sometimes she
sends a surprise.

I carried the box into the house and cleared a space for it on
the dining room table. Inside was a package wrapped in shiny
blue paper and tied with a white cotton ribbon printed with blue
letters: "Gien Boutique." A heavy paper card embossed with a
purple iris was wedged beside the gift. I opened it and read.

Linda had been in Paris. She'd seen the cup and it made her
smile and remember days when we could quote a paragraph from
The Little Prince at a moment's notice. She hoped the cup would
make me smile, too.

I carefully unwrapped my new treasure. It was a teacup and
saucer decorated with color illustrations from *The Little Prince*. It

did make me smile. Later, I'd brew some tea and take it to my desk. I'd drink slowly from the cup and write Linda a letter.

I looked at the clock; time to pick up the children. Eager to share news of the surprise package, I walked to the car with a spring in my step.

~

Old friends are the common thread that stitch the old year to the new, that add a bit of sparkle to the dark times. They hold the fabric of our lives together when it threatens to unravel before our eyes.

Like threads in a tapestry, they weave in and out of our days. Some infuse design and color for years, continuing until the end. Others burst into the pattern, flashes of interest that come and go.

Jesus, you were a friend. You talked and listened, laughed and wept with those who were your companions. There were special ones who rejoiced with you, and held your tired spirit when you grew weary. With them you shared food and home and fellowship. Bless those long-time friends who are part of the fabric of my life.

A Gift of Tea

~

The ornament of a house is the friends who frequent it.
Ralph Waldo Emerson

There is nothing like a cup of tea with an old friend. When Rita wakes up, her first task is to stoke the fire in the woodburner. I get up, check the thermostat, and throw a blanket around my shoulders before putting the tea kettle on the stove. While I get the children ready for school and onto their buses, she's miles away, feeding cows or checking the chicken house.

The last bus pulls away. With a push, the back door shuts, closing out the winter wind. I reach for the half-pint canning jars stacked neatly on the counter. Filled with herbs from her garden, they were a Christmas gift from Rita. I unscrew the lid of the jar labeled "applemint" and crush the dried leaves between my fingers. Wonderful smells of mint and summer gardens fill the kitchen.

Right about now my friend is probably sitting down to a cup of coffee. She knows I prefer tea. We cradle the mugs with our hands. Then we lay our hot hands on our neck or cheeks, spreading the heat. I can't see her, but I know that is what she is doing. I picture Rita in the gardens, picking the mint and herbs; tying them with string and hanging them upside down to dry; then packing them up and sending them in our Christmas package. A gift of tea, summer, and herself.

~

In today's mobile society, friends are often far away. Yet the spirit is not bound by time and space. Miles mean little to love that is shared. A jar of mint leaves called me to take time and sit with a dear friend. So, I made the cup of tea and sat at the table. I spent time with Rita in her summer gardens, in the dark drying places, in the bright kitchen where she packed the jars.

God, help me to hear the call of people and things and events you put into my day. You call from eternity, and invite me to sit for a while with you there.

"Just-in-Time" Companions

*The most called upon prerequisite of a friend
is an accessible ear.²*
Maya Angelou

Around the dining room table we sit: five friends who find times during the year to share coffee and conversation. We met as many mothers do: at our children's school. Years later, our children are in different places and involved in different activities. Our schedules don't mesh as often as they once did. We still manage to be together occasionally, laughing, sharing stories, and helping one another put our problems in perspective.

"I thought I was the only one who couldn't keep up with the mountains of clothes in the basement. You all seem so much more organized."

"Are you kidding? I race down to the basement and throw in a quick load of undershirts while he's in the shower. I run up and yell through the door that they're not quite dry yet. Then, I run back downstairs and hope they'll be finished before he is. It's the only time I'm glad he takes long showers."

"Really! Nothing wakes me faster than his mumbling 'Where are my socks?' at five in the morning. 'They're in the laundry basket,' I say. 'I didn't get them sorted out yet. Just a minute.' Then I stumble downstairs in my nightgown and bare feet, hoping to find a matching pair."

"My husband calls it 'Just-in-Time laundry.'"

We laugh and have another cup of coffee.

It's a female thing. If our husbands had been listening, they would have thought we were complaining, or asking for answers. They would offer to "fix" the problems. But we didn't want someone to tell us how to solve our laundry woes. Often, we don't want something solved. We may not even want it changed. But to cope with the myriad of humble tasks and challenges that fill our days, we need to talk. Women friends need to sit around a table and listen, laugh, and know they are not alone in ordinary struggles.

~

Holy One, our ears are like your own. You listen and hold, giving strength by your Presence alone. Sometimes you listen through my friends. Sometimes I throw my voice to you in frustration. Sometimes I cry my heart out quietly on my pillow. Sometimes I hold a child in my lap and rock and send my thoughts to you in silence. You are always listening. You help me remember I live none of my humble life alone.

THE CONTEST
∾

*To have a good friend is one of the highest delights
of life; to be a good friend is one of the noblest
and most difficult undertakings.*
Anonymous

My daughter Emily had been writing stories since she was five. It was something special we shared together. She would talk excitedly about entering the school's young author contest someday.

The year she was finally old enough, she refused to enter. I was bewildered. "Why won't you try? I thought you'd love to go!"

Her eyes clouded as she evaded my questions and she dashed upstairs.

When I followed, she was in bed, tears dripping down her face.

"I'm sorry, Mom. I don't want to disappoint you. I just don't want to this year. That's all."

I gave her a hug and kiss. Sighing, I walked downstairs knowing this was one more in a growing list of mishandled parenting opportunities.

That evening her brother Josh filled me in. "Mom, she just doesn't want to go up against Angie."

Emily and Angie had been best friends since meeting at age four. They shared a variety of interests and were comfortable with the differences. Once I'd picked up Angie from kindergarten to celebrate Emily's birthday with us. She sat at the table, making a birthday card. Studying dinosaurs that adorned a birthday banner, she stopped coloring.

"Emily loves dinosaurs," she observed. "I hate them." She

returned to coloring. "But that's OK," she added. "Best friends don't have to like the same things."

Their friendship was a gift, I had told my daughter. Emily and Angie, looking out for each other. I thought about what Josh had said.

"Really Mom. That's why she won't write a story."

Before long I found out how correct he was. Rather than judging stories written especially for the contest, the girls' teacher had chosen a contestant based on his observations of each student's work for the entire year. He had chosen Emily.

Emily was torn. She had deliberately not written a story for the contest so that her friend might have a better chance of winning. "I'd like to be in the contest, but Angie really wanted to be in it. I don't mind waiting."

At last Emily decided she wouldn't go unless her friend was happy with the arrangement. The next day at school Angie, of course, said she was.

~

The writing contests and the honors paled beside the lesson these two young friends had lived out for the few of us who knew what went on beneath the surface. They were best friends, willing to sacrifice their own ambitions for the other. Quietly and without resentment. Emily told me she was sorry for disappointing me. Lord, who disappointed whom?

TRANSPARENCY OF FRIENDSHIP

*My friends have made the story of my life. In a
thousand ways they have turned my limitations
into beautiful privileges, and enabled me
to walk serene and happy in the shadow
cast by my deprivation.*[3]
Helen Keller

Awakened by a throbbing pain in my knee, I stared at the red numerals glowing from across the room: 2 A.M. Unable to put weight on the knee, I inched out of bed, hopped into the living room and flopped into the rocker.

I tried to massage the pain away, gently pushing and probing the sensitive spots with my fingers. Cautiously flexing the joint, I extended my leg and then let it return slowly to a resting position.

Usually, some circumstance precipitated problems with my knee: a twist on the way down the hill to the creek, or too many round trips on the three flights of stairs at school. This time, I could think of nothing.

In the morning, the doctor suggested using crutches for a day or two. I mentally ran through a list of friends who might own a pair. Maybe someone with a son who plays football. A phone call confirmed my hunch. Amy had a pair and could bring them over after dropping off her children at school.

I hopped into the kitchen and unlocked the door. Unwashed dishes were piled in the sink. Glancing into the living room, I saw a basket of laundry waiting to be folded at the end of the couch. Back in bed, I began to feel uncomfortable about Amy coming into such a mess. My dresser was cluttered with a half-read novel, two pairs of socks, and an assortment of receipts I'd been meaning to file away.

I looked in the mirror. A slightly wild-looking woman blinked back at me. I ran a comb through my hair, rested back on the pillows, and waited.

A car door slammed shut and Amy was knocking at the door.

"I'm here!" her cheerful voice announced.

"Come on in, just don't look around," I called out.

She brought the crutches into the bedroom and began to ply me with questions. We laughed at the improbability of the situation, wondered about the headlines, and swapped stories about our children. I forgot about the dishes in the sink and my bedraggled appearance, and Amy didn't notice.

~

Weakness is humbling. We can't present a facade. The fragility and imperfections of human nature stick out like pimples on a face. What a grace are friends who respond to our need and love us as we are. Is that how God is? I hope so.

MY SISTER, MY FRIEND

For there is no friend like a sister
In calm and stormy weather;
To cheer one on the tedious way,
To fetch one if one goes astray,
To lift one if one totters down,
To strengthen while one stands.[4]
Christina Rossetti

Sleepily, I wave out the door as the school bus pulls away. The tea kettle whistles on the stove and I pour the steamy water over the bag in my cup. Spicy, sweet smells fill the kitchen.

I breathe slowly, pulling the soothing vapors deep into my lungs. Worry had kept sleep away most of the night. Parenting requires wisdom and faith I don't always have. In darker moments, I wonder if I have any at all.

Sipping tea helps me wake up, but the uneasy feeling of an unresolved problem remains. It will lurk on the edges of my mind, pushing out more productive thoughts and sabotaging the work of the day. I have yet to conquer worry.

I dial my older sister's number and the phone rings. I hope Jan is there. We chose similar paths: marriage, children, and staying at home. The phone is still ringing. AT&T doesn't mind that we live states apart, but I wish we could share tea and a conversation in person.

"Hello."

"Jan? It's Mary."

"Hi! How are you doing?" She misses close family, and is glad for the call. I picture her in the kitchen, probably surrounded by the remains of a big family's breakfast. Suddenly, I feel foolish bringing up my little concerns. People are dying in civil wars all over the world while others are losing jobs or are homeless. Why can little things trouble me so?

"Oh, OK. I wanted to talk with you about something."

She listens.

"Yes, I hear you."

I know she does. Her path has challenges, too. We talk about options. Having been a wife and mother longer than I, she shares her experience in similar situations. I listen, mentally taking notes. But solutions are not what I really need. I need the uncovering of faith and the hope that flows from it. Sometimes it gets buried under the rush and clutter of my life. Jan's certitude helps dig it out.

"You know, Mary, it will fall into place in the long run. God's hand is in this, too."

I know that. Why do I feel the need to sift through all the details and make everything all right? How can I assume that the responsibility for solutions is all mine? Trust stirs within and begins to push away the anxiety that had been seeping into my spirit like cold leaking through cracks around a door.

"Wouldn't it be good if we lived closer?"

I smile. Yes, it would be great.

My big sister seemed like a grown-up to me when I was a child. I was just starting high school when she graduated from college. I admired her friends and was flattered when they noticed me. We shared a bedroom with a grandmother and a younger sister, but we didn't play much. Sometimes we fought. My mother would shake her head and say to the three of us: "There is nothing like a sister. Someday you'll be glad you have each other."

She was right.

~

No matter the distance. No matter the time. Whatever the topic. Whatever the problem. My sisters are people I can count on. Bound by best-friendship as much as by blood, our lives twine together through the years.

Lord, thank you for the gift of my sisters. They are often the ones you use to touch my heart and quiet my spirit.

FOR ANDREW

He is thy friend, who is thy friend at all times; of a brother's love there is no test like adversity.
Proverbs 17:17 KJV

"We're going to see Andrew," the couple said, driving five hours to visit their elderly friend. The three of them have been each other's support through the Depression and the wars. They have celebrated weddings and births, and grieved the deaths of friends. Now they are old and Andrew is alone. A few hundred miles would not keep them from being companions through this part of life.

I watched them go to help Andrew pay his bills and to look for a home. Sometimes he wouldn't remember who they were but they kept going. They helped him pack and move and clean the apartment.

They worried about the adjustment, but the move has been good for Andrew. He is brighter and happier than he has been in years. When they visit now, the three of them sit and remember the old days. They admire the crafts decorating his room that he's made in recreation classes. When evening comes they eat together in the dining room and laugh and ponder life's twists and turns.

"You don't know what it means to see him so well," the wife says.

I don't, but I can guess. She is glowing.

~

What a blessing these people are to one another. Are such friendships made anymore? Friendships that last through scores of years and draw friends together over hundreds of miles to care for one another?

Lord, help me make time for my friends now. We are all busy. Sometimes the commitment of true friendship seems impossible to maintain. Living a lifestyle on the run, we often pass on the road or in the stores. But these are the times we will be remembering one day. We'll have memories that will make us laugh and cry. When I am old, I will want to share those times with friends like Andrew's.

BEFRIENDING THE LONELY

*A young village girl told me, when I am about to
talk to anyone, I picture to myself Jesus Christ and
how gracious and friendly he was to everyone.*[5]
John Vianney

"Sara! Hello! How are you and the boys today?"

The young mother turned her attention from the grocery list
and the three-year-old sitting in the cart to the lady coming
toward her past rows of cereal boxes.

"Oh, fine, thanks. Just stocking up. The cupboard's pretty
low."

Sara smiled and began pushing her cart up the aisle.

"Well, that happens with two growing boys. My son just called
yesterday. He's in Florida, you know. I did tell you he got a job,
didn't I?"

"Yes." Sara smiled again and leaned on her cart.

While the lady continued her story, Sara tried to look attentive.
She was thinking of ways to politely move on. The lady was nice
enough. Sara just didn't enjoy her company or her conversation.

"...And then Jeff said he had had enough of those dogs next
door. He thought he'd moved into a quiet neighborhood and
now this. Can you imagine?"

"Hmmm." Sara nodded and wondered why they always ran
into her at the store. She opened a bag of animal crackers and
handed a few to the three-year-old who had begun chewing on
the bag. Her other son had found a cereal box with a silver holo-
gram on the front promising an incredible prize inside. He put it
into the cart.

"I really must get going before the boys fill the cart for me!"

"Well, yes. Sorry. Come for coffee, Sara. I'd love to have you."

Sara smiled again and escaped around the end of the breakfast food aisle and into pet supplies.

"Are we getting a dog?"

"No, Michael." Just getting away, she thought to herself. She felt guilty. The woman must be lonely, always asking her for coffee. But Sara didn't think she could stand another story about Jeff and his troubles. She had enough to keep her busy. A cart rolled behind her down the aisle. "Why, Sara! I didn't know you had a dog!"

~

Mother Teresa says she sees Jesus' face in everyone she meets and cares for. How does she do it? I struggle with loving those closest to me, let alone strangers or people I do not care for.

Jesus, do you really come to us in all those we meet? How would I react to my husband's late return from work if I looked at him and saw you, tired and weary from your labor? What if I knew your struggle to be understood as I hold a child in my lap? Our family life would be transformed.

Could I possibly see you rejected and scorned in those who do not fit in my circles, in my world? Do the immigrants or the homeless show me the face of a child-God living in exile, or a man-God with no place to lay his head? Jesus, help me understand your presence in those who fill my world.

Helping Hands

~

*She opens her arms to the poor and extends her hands to
the needy.... She is clothed with strength and dignity; she
can laugh at the days to come.... Her children arise and
call her blessed; her husband also, and he praises her.*
Proverbs 31:20, 25, 28

My mother and her friends taught me how to be a friend.
They washed dishes and heaped food on plates whenever
there was a wedding, graduation, or first communion. They took
food to grieving families.

Most mothers worked at home then. They were a neighborhood community running groups of teens to the high school, or
leading Girl Scout troops. They were ready to bake an extra cake,
or welcome another child or two for the night. They stretched
their schedules and their budgets and made room.

Stretching a schedule is more difficult when working for someone else, but mothers still do it. The cakes may be store bought,
but mothers still take food to families who have lost someone
they love. Their homes still stretch to hold extra children.

~

Surely, Jesus watched his mother carry food to an ailing neighbor, and volunteer to watch a few extra children. She helped cook
and clean for friends who were celebrating weddings, or mourn-
ing a death. Mothers have always been doing those things and
children have been watching. I'm glad. I want my daughters to
say that their mother and her friends taught them about being a
friend.

ON THE FRINGE

*Loneliness and the feeling of being unwanted
is the most terrible poverty.*
Mother Teresa

She sat by herself on the edge of the grass, watching a softball game. I'd seen her at recess before. She was usually alone wandering the perimeter of the school yard. Occasionally she'd bend down and examine an interesting rock. If it was particularly nice, she'd shove it into her pocket before moving on.

I went over and sat beside her.

"Who's winning?"

"Oh, the usual. Those girls play together all the time. They're good."

"You like softball?"

"Yeah." Pause. "I don't know. I mean, they have their teams. They just don't like me, I guess."

"What about Julie? I've seen you talking with her."

"Oh, Julie is nice. But, see, her friends don't like me, so she's kinda stuck. If she plays with me, she loses them. If she sticks with them, well, I guess I lose her." Pause. "That's OK. Hey, I found some great rocks today. Wanna see?"

I nodded and she emptied her pocket. I fingered the five stones. Most were quartz, but she had one good fossil. I watched her face when Julie and her friends walked by. Julie waved. The girl's face lit up for a moment before she looked back down at the stones she had placed in my hand.

~

Growing up and learning about friendship is not easy. I remember tough days on the school playground. I've been on the edge. Less frequently, I've been like Julie and her friends. Both places can be painful.

Jesus was on both sides, too. He was sought after, a good name to drop. He was also nailed to a cross. Yet he had no trouble reaching out to those on the edge. He took each person where they were and related to them honestly. That is how he takes me.

Jesus, help me be an example of compassion to my own children. Bless the children who struggle. Bless those on the fringes who long for companions, and those who hesitate to reach out.

PART THREE

HOMEFRONT

Years ago, when I first started writing a monthly column for our diocesan newspaper, my children were young and kept me busy at home. Trips to the downtown office were an opportunity to walk in another milieu for a while. The people at work there connected me to a sphere of thought and ideas swirling somewhere beyond my immediate world of toddlers, diapers, and home.

First I would deliver the copy and visit with staff. We talked about the news, the column, and interesting happenings in our lives. Ever encouraging, the editor was happy to answer questions about copyrights, column length, and deadlines. When the dream of actually being published seemed beyond reach, his confidence in my writing bolstered hope.

Next I usually stopped in at the Family Life Bureau down the hall to share a cup of coffee with the director. He would tell me about new books he thought I'd like or a convention he had attended. Still, the conversation usually returned to family. His children were also young, and there were stories to share. One day Mark said he didn't know why more people didn't think of family life when they thought about works of mercy or the Beatitudes. "You don't have to be a missionary to feed the hungry or to be a peacemaker," he would say. I agreed. Family provided abundant opportunity.

Now, my children are fast growing. My life is tied in many concrete ways to the world I watched from behind stacks of laundry. Teaching, writing, and speaking have been broadening experiences. But the change has not come without a price.

Juggling a number of roles sometimes proved to be more of a challenge than I wanted. During the weeks I taught, my eighth-grade daughter rode home with a friend who lived near the elementary school where I worked. I picked her up on my way home. Standing inside the kitchen, waiting for Emily to gather her books, I'd smell dinner cooking and remember that nothing had been planned for our own. I watched my friend with her two-year-old and envied her the luxury of the time she spent with him. To my amazement, I began to long for time to stay home, cook, and make our house more hospitable again.

Distance provides perspective. While I enjoyed my work, I had to admit that my connections with the world seemed somehow superficial at times, full of fatigue and busyness. By comparison, my friend's connections—and those I had formed during my years as a stay-at-home mom—seemed far deeper and more profound.

A mother's call plunges her into life, intimately intertwines her spirit with those of her spouse and children. A mother's life is often lived moment by moment. Event by event. Chore by chore. Since she cannot see the result of all those moments strung together, her call can seem unimportant. She sees only the laundry basket emptied, a dinner fixed, a knee bandaged.

But the cross is also the blessing. Being immersed in serving life moment by moment, the mother also serves the Author of life. God is met in the moment, as ordinary as it may be. She, like a monk who goes to the monastery not to escape the world but to be one with it, is connected to it through Jesus, the root of all being. On the homefront, through her family, the mother touches and is touched by the Lord. Through him she is involved in the world and its redemption. She will never know the ways it is accomplished. That is the Mystery of the Incarnation.

A HOUSEFUL OF GIFTS

∾

When you tidy your house, think that it is Mine and
you will make it more beautiful. When you prepare
your meals think that it is to honor Me.[1]
Gabrielle Bossis

The mundane chores of keeping a family and household running can seem so unimportant. How much intelligence is
needed to measure a scoop of laundry detergent or to wash a sink
full of dishes? Besides, housework is never done. Dishes always
need washing and clothes just get dirty again. My distaste for
housework is no secret. I've always said if I was wealthy enough, I
wouldn't hesitate to hire someone else to do it.

So, my children looked at me with disbelief when they came
home from school one day and found me cheerfully scrubbing
away. I smiled at them and dunked my rag into the bucket of hot,
soapy water. Wringing it out, I began on the next cupboard.

"When **is** spring cleaning, anyway?" asked a puzzled first
grader.

"Not now. This is December!" her sister answered.

"Well, this is as close to spring cleaning as I've been in years,"
I said.

"I can't believe you want to do this, Mom. I mean, you're in a
good mood and everything. Are you going to clean the whole
house?"

I revealed my plans: Two weeks of Advent would be given
over to cleaning and getting the house ready for the holidays. I'd
see how far I could get.

Each day I looked forward to the next project. I enjoyed stay-

71

ing home and out of the shopping frenzy. I delighted in the simple satisfaction of seeing a clean wall where a smudge of fingerprints had been. Sometimes I put on a favorite piece of music. Other times, I was content with the quiet. Once, while doing dishes, I composed a line or two of poetry in my head.

Housework took on a new dimension. There was no hurry. It was a luxury to have time to myself to think or pray. When folding clothes, I thought of the people who lived in them. I prayed for the children at school and for my husband at work. Scrubbing and finding places for odds and ends that had been laying on counters for months, I thought of friends who would come over during the holidays. We would share food and conversation in these places I was making ready.

After two weeks, three rooms had been cleaned from top to bottom. I bought a poinsettia and placed it on a dining room buffet unusually free of clutter. Gazing at it while drinking a cup of tea, I realized how much I would have missed had we been wealthy enough to hire someone else to do the cleaning.

～

Lord, help me see the chance to serve others as I go about my housework. Instead of begrudging the effort and resenting the time it demands, open my heart to see these tasks as a chance to nurture those I love. Our home can be a welcoming refuge from the demands and stresses of the world. The work that is done here may be done with a generous spirit that will spill over and envelop those who enter. My house will never be perfectly ordered or spotless. But it can be comfortable and warm. I am clothing you, comforting you in my family and friends. These chores are a gift that give me moments of peace to withdraw from the world and remind myself that we are called to be servants. Humble tasks are channels of great grace.

LITURGY OF THE HOURS

*The different activities of our daily lives are not
distraction from prayer, but rather
the rich soil for prayer.²*
Edward Hays

The house is quiet except for the stirring of a baby. Her mother does not need to look at the clock. She knows it is time for the 2:00 A.M. feeding. Rousing herself from the warm cocoon of blankets, she shuffles into the nursery. Deftly, her hands scoop the infant from its crib. Talking in quiet, mother tones, she soothes the child while changing her diaper and replacing the little terry sleeper.

Smells of sweet baby breath and soft skin fill the mother's nostrils as she settles into the living-room rocker to nurse her child. The early-morning feeding isn't always so peaceful. Sometimes the baby is demanding and fussy. But always there are a few quiet moments when the child begins to suckle. The mother rocks gently and gazes out the window into the night.

~

In monasteries the world over monks and sisters rise early for Matins. As a child, I was instructed never to speak to a priest if he had his head bowed over his prayer book. I might interrupt his praying the Divine Office. It seemed very mysterious to me.

It isn't mysterious anymore. Mothers, too, pray a liturgy of hours. Their matins are the 2:00 A.M. feedings; the hours, morning prayer and making breakfast and getting children off to school. Vespers are preparing meals and saying grace before them. Compline is bedtime stories and prayers. In homes everywhere, mothers rise together and give of themselves to nourish the new life God has created with them. In the evenings they gather their children and help them close their day with peace and with God.

In middle-class homes, in grass huts, in homeless shelters, in adobe buildings, in ghettos and cities and farm houses, the mothers pray matins and compline with their babes.

THE VISIT

∾

But his father ordered his servants, "Quickly bring the finest robe and put it on him; put a ring on his finger and sandals on his feet. Take the fattened calf and slaughter it. Let us celebrate with a feast."
Luke 15:22-23

My mother amazes me. At seventy-six she still possesses an ample supply of the spirit that helped her raise five children. Smells of spaghetti sauce and lemon meringue pies spilled out the door when I stopped by yesterday. Mom was bustling around the house, cooking and cleaning.

"Who's coming?" I asked as we sat at the kitchen table.

"Jan and the children will be down Wednesday." She smiled in anticipation. "I've got to get this house ready."

The house looked good to me. I made the token objection, knowing it would be ignored.

"Don't work so hard, Mom. We come to visit you, not the house!"

"I know. I know. But I want it to be comfortable."

Never trusting the "clean" of a sponge mop, she still scrubs the kitchen floor on her hands and knees. Every bed will have fresh sheets. The pantry will be stocked with the grandchildren's favorite breakfast foods, and she will stay up late baking cookies.

Her children worry. She doesn't. She wants her home to envelop her family in a warm embrace. Cheerful, expectant, stocked with everything we could need, it mirrors her own heart.

∼

The desire to nurture and comfort does not diminish with age. My mother wants to provide a place of rest, acceptance, and love now, as always. Her body grows older but her spirit remains selfless, ready to offer herself completely.

Humbled by her generosity, I recall the truth her giving reflects: From all time, God desires to lavish us with his extravagant love. To protest as unworthy is of no avail. This unthinkable gift is freely given.

GRACE IN THE KITCHEN

He makes grass grow for the cattle, and plants for
man to cultivate—bringing forth food from the earth:
wine that gladdens the heart of man, oil to make his
face shine, and bread that sustains his heart.
Psalm 104:14-15

I especially enjoy preparing dinner when the menu depends on a garden's yield. "Creative cooking," I call it. One day in particular I had planned an eggplant casserole. As I walked into the kitchen, morning sun shone through the window. It fell across a variety of vegetables jumbled on the counter. Purple. Yellow. Red. Green. Piercingly intense, like pure hues of a stained-glass window, their colors commanded notice, and reverence for the Creator.

I stood quietly for some time before moving to pick them up. The eggplant was first. Its tough, satiny skin parted to reveal spongy flesh, specked with seeds. I salted the slices and put them between paper towels with a weight on top. Next, the tomatoes were skinned and put in a pot on the stove to simmer.

Dicing the tiny onions made tears stream down my face. Then came the yellow and green peppers. I cut one in half across the middle, the other lengthwise to see different patterns before adding them all to the pot. Finally, I reached for the spices. The pungent smells of basil and oregano flooded the kitchen. Two cloves of garlic finished the sauce.

Alternating layers of eggplant, sauce, and cheese, I had dinner ready to bake. I had said morning prayer in my kitchen church.

~

How many meals do I make in a year? Cooking is one of a mother's permanent occupations. On some days, getting food on the table is anything but a reflective exercise. When it requires opening cans and boxes, or peeling plastic film from a frozen entree, the opportunity to revere its Creator is often lost.

Lord, thank you for the gift of produce fresh from gardens, or bought in the store just as it was taken from the fields. When I see it, I recall the beauty and variety of creation. I am mindful of your presence. Touching it causes me to remember that life is a gift, dependent on other life to survive.

Once I read about a woman who prayed as she cooked each meal for her family. She hoped the food would be strength for their bodies and that her love in fixing it would nourish their souls. Let my cooking be a source of grace for my family.

THE ONE WITH
THE VISION

*Now the earth was a formless void, there was chaos over
the deep, and God's spirit hovered over the water.*
Genesis 1:1-2

Sidestepping the ruins of a stuffed toy and a building block tower, I headed toward the dining room. Underneath the table sat a bowl of water and little dishes filled with scraps of paper. Play food was everywhere. Sighing, I gathered up the mess. After disposing of the paper and dumping the water in the sink, I walked into the living room. Little piles of torn paper were dotting the couch. I daydreamed about living alone in a tidy, little cottage where the only messes were ones I made myself.

"Mom! Quick! Look at this!"

My son was calling from his bedroom.

"It's a chocolate milk maker, and it really works!"

Carefully, he carried the precariously built contraption into the kitchen. After it was safely on the counter, he got out milk, chocolate syrup, and a glass. It worked. After five minutes it had pumped a cup of chocolate milk into a glass sitting in the middle of a milk and syrup puddle.

"Here, try it." With the pride and aplomb of Henry Ford watching the first car roll off the assembly line, he handed me the dripping glass.

"Mmmm. Tastes great," I confirmed his expectations.

Suddenly, a cry came from the living room.

"What happened to my pies? Who took my pies?"

Josh and I exchanged puzzled glances. My three-year-old was anxiously examining the couch and crawling under the dining room table. In a flash of recognition, I realized I was the culprit. They had looked like piles of torn paper to me.

Living with young children taught me that order is in the vision of things. Where I saw messes, they saw pies, kitty houses, and projects almost done. Inventors, scientists, and artists do the same. They let numbers and ideas play in their minds. They spread out parts or sketches, arranging and rearranging until they discover the order that gives them meaning. Then, the equations give name to some glory of creation, the colors and shapes reflect life. The idea becomes reality.

We still have messes; they just look different. Instead of blocks we have lathes, tools, and bins of "parts." The kitty houses have been replaced by classrooms for dolls. Instead of pies, we are baking clay sculptures. Manuscripts spill out of my office and pile on the dining room table. I know it's not a mess. It's a book in process!

~

Lord, grant me patience with the messes in my life. We all need freedom to experiment, be creative, and make mistakes. We need time to lay out the elements in our world and see how they fit together.

You are patient with me, using the circumstances of my life, and the people in it to gradually draw me to yourself. Sometimes it is a beautiful unfolding. Sometimes it is as dark and dry as a moonless desert night. It is often messy. Order is in the vision of things. You are the One with the vision.

OUR PLACE OF PRAYER

ॐ

The road to the sacred leads through the secular.[3]
Abraham Heschel

A friend who is a priest shared a story of an unusual house
blessing. Having had many requests to bless homes, he
arrived at this particular one with a ritual and prayers ready. The
family, however, had their own idea.

They met him at the front door and took him on a tour of the
house. At each room they stopped and shared with him the
meanings that space had in their lives.

To one the kitchen was a gathering place. There the children
first touched base after school. They grabbed a snack and
recounted events of the day. Another saw the kitchen as a place
that welcomed friends, a place where food that nourished both
body and soul was prepared: Cakes for celebrations, special dinners, and hot soup for an ailing child. So much more than just
sustenance comes from the kitchen.

A child's bedroom was a place where he could close the door
and be alone. He could read there, do his homework, or just
think. It offered him space to retreat when he was at odds with
the rest of the family. In his room he could decide when and how
to rejoin the usual activity and be reconciled.

The younger children's bedroom was a magical place where
gerbils and tadpoles and hermit crabs lived. A glow-in-the-dark
moon kept the girls company at night. The room could be anything from a school to a medieval forest. It offered them a world
to explore.

The parents knew their bedroom was a place of sharing life. In
that room they celebrated their love. Children were conceived

there. Hurt, anger, and fears were healed there with tears, late night conversations, and prayer. They could be alone, together, in their bedroom.

Even the bathroom was to be blessed. It was the place to make ready, the last stop before entering the flow of life at work, at home, or at school. One parent reflected on the gift of water to cleanse, refresh, and heal. For another, the bathroom was full of memories: watching a daughter examine her hair before a first date, or a son execute his first shave.

"They shared their house with me," said our friend. "I blessed what I knew was already holy."

~

Lord, our home is our family's domestic church. Its spaces are our places of prayer. In our home we celebrate significant events in our lives. Here the liturgy of family life plays out. We encounter you in the midst of it all.

When I clean the counter and place a vase of snapdragons where everyone can enjoy them, it is like putting flowers on your altar. For here in this home we most often offer ourselves up for each other and for you.

Rushin' and Runnin'

ॐ

The reason why we don't take time is a feeling that we have to keep moving. This is a real sickness. Today time is a commodity, and for each one of us time is mortgaged....We must approach the whole idea of time in a new way.[4]
Thomas Merton

"I'm beginning to dread Tuesdays," I thought to myself as I straightened the stack of magazines on the end table. When I wasn't working at my part-time job, Tuesday mornings were a good time to catch up on housework. But once school was out for the day, my running began.

First, I'd drop one child off for piano lessons before taking another to the local college for a class. Then I'd pick up my budding pianist and come home to feed her and her brother. Next I would take him to the high school and her to ballet. By then my other daughter's class would be finished. When our family was younger, I looked at mothers who ran like this and promised myself I never would. What happened?

I sank into a chair and fingered the shells we kept on the table. They remind us of summers at the ocean. I thought of our friend, Page, and a conversation we once had had at the beach.

Seventy-seven years of living, loving, and learning have made her an engaging companion. The wisdom she has acquired slips as smoothly and unconsciously from her lips as her Southern drawl. We had been watching children playing night games on the beach. A full moon silvered the sea and the foam glowed from within.

"Time," she had mused. "The children need time with their families. But everybody's rushin' around so. Runnin' here and

83

runnin' there. Making money. Lots of 'em have to. Hardly any family anymore." She shook her head. "I wonder what they'll have when they grow up?"

As I sat in the living room, I tried to remember more of the conversation. Our family was surely "runnin' here and runnin' there." My husband often worked late. I got caught up in projects at school. The children had lessons and teams and classes. I didn't remember what we were hurrying after, or what we were losing in the pursuit. I wished I were back on the beach. I'd ask Page.

~

Lord, my life has become what I never intended it to be: an unending string of appointments, activities, and responsibilities that leave little time for anything else. Relationships, prayer, and reflection get lost in the bustle. What good are things or experiences when we have no time to enjoy them or reflect on their meaning? The world tempts us with so much that seems good. Perhaps striving for more than my share is leading to this feeling of discontent.

Some running is inevitable. It is part of family life. Help me to choose wisely what fills my time. Help me remember the importance of prayer and relationships. They provide balance and perspective as I negotiate the demands of motherhood.

THE QUALITY OF MERCY

∽

Blessed are the merciful: for they shall obtain mercy.
Matthew 5:7 KJV

Sitting in the living room rocker, I could hear crying coming from the girls' bedroom. A few moments later a door slammed and the light footsteps of my youngest came running down the stairs. She plopped herself on my lap and wiped her nose across her sleeve.

"What's the problem?" I asked.

She looked at me with teary eyes and began the explanation. "She was yelling at me and I was yelling at her and then she told me I couldn't play with that little dog I gave her, so I said 'OK, but you can't use my dolls then...'"

She paused for a breath and wiped her nose again. In a quiet voice, she continued.

"I called her names."

"Did you tell her you were sorry?"

"No, not yet."

She paused again. Fighting off a fresh flow of tears she added: "Do you think she'll accept?"

Her question caught me by surprise. I hadn't considered the possibility of her not being forgiven. So honest and vulnerable, she wanted to make things right between herself and her sister, but she knew it wasn't all up to her. She could ask for forgiveness, but her sister would have to give it.

∽

Admitting sin and asking forgiveness exposes our fragile selves to the possibility of hurt and rejection. Thank you, Jesus, for gently receiving my contrite heart and being quick to forgive my transgressions. Blessed are those in my life and in our world who reflect your compassionate mercy.

TIME FOR LOVE

*Do any human beings ever realize life while they
live it—every, every minute?[5]*
Thornton Wilder

After a long day, I was finally home fixing dinner. My mind
was still at school, going over plans for tomorrow's science
project. I barely heard my daughter's voice.

"Mo-om! I said I was making a house for Annie upstairs and I
want to show you. Can you come up?"

"Sorry, honey. I didn't hear you."

She repeated her question.

"So, you're making a house for your doll?"

"I'm using that big box Dad brought home. I put designs on
the walls and made a table out of a littler box. Come on, I'll show
you."

"Not right now. I'm finishing dinner."

"After that?"

"No. I want to get out of these clothes. Grandma and Grandpa are coming for dinner. They'll be here soon."

"Grandma and Grandpa are coming?" she asked.

"Mm-hmm."

"You know what I love about Grandma and Grandpa?" my
daughter asked.

"What," I answered absentmindedly, stirring the spaghetti
sauce.

"They always have time."

~

When I was growing up, my grandmother lived with us. We called her Becky. She was always ready for a game of canasta, and she entertained us with stories of her childhood. She was accepting, unthreatening, and always had time. When Mom and I were not seeing eye to eye, Becky was the one I could talk to.

My parents are that gift of presence now to my children. They delight in one another. There is always time for a story, a walk, a game. They "cook" on pretend stoves made out of cardboard boxes or shoot pool in the basement. When they are feeling unsure of themselves, the children can count on Grandma and Grandpa for affirmation. They love the children just as they are.

It is good to know that God is like that. He has time. He delights in us. When we feel unlovable or unforgivable, God loves and forgives.

"LOVE JESUS WHERE YOU ARE..."

We can do no great things;
only small things with great love.
Mother Teresa

My husband and I sat with hundreds of others gathered to hear Mother Teresa speak. Scanning the bare stage, I scrutinized the curtains for some sign of movement, some signal that she was about to appear.

Suddenly, she was there. The spotlights converged on her small, sari-draped frame. Had she not spoken a word, every person there would still have riveted his or her attention on Mother Teresa.

It was not how she looked or what she said that plumbed our hearts and seeded them with hope. It wasn't her at all. It was the tremendous reality of God's Presence radiating from a woman whose life and love had made her a clear vessel for it. It was like looking at a glass box and seeing the treasure within it. That Presence became tangible through Mother Teresa. People hungry to know what they often struggle to believe experienced God's promise: I am with you.

Looking back on that evening, I cannot remember many specific things she said. The sense of Presence is what remains with me. She spoke simply about her work. She talked of serving Jesus in the poorest of the poor, and of poverty's many faces. As she spoke, God stirred the desire for himself that he has placed in our hearts. I, too, wanted to know Jesus as she did.

Someone, giving voice to that yearning, asked what she could do. She worked with wealthy children. Should she leave that job and serve the poor instead?

In a gentle but firm voice, Mother Teresa answered her. *Stay,* she said. *You are not serving money, you are serving children. They are Jesus, too. There are many kinds of poverty. Love Jesus where you are.*

~

After experiencing the power of God's Presence in Mother Teresa, I wondered what the people of his day felt when they encountered Jesus walking the earth. Wherever he was, crowds followed. God's Presence in Mother Teresa drew many to her. After the talk, she went into the foyer. People pressed closer, hoping to touch her. Hoping, perhaps, that that touch would bring them closer to God.

Jesus, I long for closeness with you. Yet I wonder if my life is too ordinary to be a way to holiness. It is spent doing many small, seemingly insignificant things. I don't do anything exceptional. I don't preach your word in the missions or care for the poor in the cities. I don't minister to the dying or rescue children from war-torn countries.

Mother Teresa's words gave me hope. She gave me a new way of understanding what you are calling me to do. Love Jesus where you are, she said. You are serving him when you serve his people.

Jesus, fill my heart with desire to love and serve you as I go about the work of being a wife and mother.

PART FOUR

❧

Good-Byes

Good-byes are always difficult. Our historic parish church is being restored. The last mass before closing it for construction was poignant. When twelve o'clock mass was over, I leaned against the pew, faced the back of church, and looked up into the loft. The organist began to play a final selection. The powerful pipe organ trembled and gave full voice to the music. I closed my eyes and let the sound wash over me. Two weeks ago that same organ had responded to the touch of another musician, Dorothy Papadakos, chief organist and composer of the Cathedral of St. John the Divine in New York City. Along with brass, strings, woodwinds, and the Lancaster chorale, it filled the church.

Strange to think of the great organ silent. For months it will be still while the church building is renewed. Protected from dust and paint, no one will wake the organ, or call music from its depths. I listened until the last notes melted into the stone walls.

Opening my eyes, I saw a man in the choir loft pointing a camera toward the sanctuary. A score of people were quietly winding their way around pews and down aisles. They stopped in front of statues. They took pictures of the gold leaf around the windows and the stone arches of the ceiling. They ran their hands along the communion rail. Some spoke quietly amongst themselves. Others remained alone, a bit red-eyed.

All lingered to drink in the sights, sounds, and smells of the church building they had known for so long. Memories of weddings and first communions, baptisms and funerals, Christmases and Easters played through their minds. For each of us there were also more private memories. Tears have been shed here. Lone pilgrims have confided their joys and sorrows to God in the big, empty church.

Saying good-bye, whatever the reason, is always bittersweet. The joy of anticipating what is to come is tinged with regret at not being able to hold on to what we already have.

Good-byes are a letting go. They are often so difficult that we sometimes choose to remain in familiar pain rather than to embrace an unknown good. Yet it is the letting go that frees us to grow and mature. The experiences, people, and places that have been part of our lives prepare us to meet new challenges.

Good-byes are a reflection of the great mystery of our Christian life: death and resurrection. Jesus said we must be like the grain of wheat that dies to bring forth new life. Good-byes are opportunities to die to some part of ourselves and to let God bring forth new life in us and in his world. Like Jesus' death, our own dying is not for personal salvation. It is the response that allows the Spirit to touch and redeem all creation.

Life's good-byes, large and small, give us the chance to let go of one thing in order to embrace something else. Since we can never know what the "something else" will bring, good-byes are opportunities to deepen our faith. We trust God will hold onto us. Our lives' good-byes help prepare us for the ultimate letting go: when we let go of our physical life, trusting God and his promise of new life.

We will always be saying good-bye to something. But along with the ending comes a beginning: we are invited to say "yes" to God. "Yes" to dying to ourselves. "Yes" to circumstances we may not understand or want. "Yes" in the face of uncertainty. "Yes" to allowing God to transform some part of our life into his life. Every "yes," every "good-bye," can become a small opening for God to transform the world. Like the pipes of the organ, we can let his breath move through us and fill the world with his song.

THE MEASURE OF A LIFE

❧

It takes three things to attain a sense of significant being:
God,
a Soul,
and a Moment.
And the three are always here.[1]
Abraham Heschel

Sitting in the crowded room, I looked at the mourners. The small-town funeral home was overflowing. My husband's grandmother had died after ninety-six full years of life. She had married a farmer who wrestled a living from clay soil. She raised fourteen children. Like other women of her time, she was quietly strong and independent. She did what she could to make a hard life bearable, seeing the good and sharing it with her children and those she knew. Her family had come to share memories, to honor her, and say good-bye.

I was young and seven months pregnant, when we first met, spending Christmas vacation with my new husband's family. I had been told that great-grandmother would be there. What gift could I take? I wrapped some jars of my canned apple butter. She accepted them with grace. She played harmonica, told stories of old times, and made me feel we were friends from the start.

I looked at the people gathered at her graveside. Her quiet life in small Ohio towns had touched many. We never know the meaning and reach of our lives.

A few days later, I thought of her long life as I walked into the back of church for another memorial service. We gathered to support the parents, family, and friends of an infant who had lived for only an hour. Praying, we sought comfort in the face of inscrutable mystery. As a mother, I know you do not need an hour of holding your child to be changed forever. The deep bond with the baby that lies on your breast is there from the moment of birth. An hour is more than enough time to feel the wrench of separation, the emptiness, the loss when the baby is gone.

One of the ministers told a story he had recently read of a boy flying a kite. Climbing high, the kite disappeared. A woman walked by and saw the boy holding the string and asked what he was doing. "Flying a kite." he replied. The lady squinted into the sky. "I can't see anything." she said. "Oh, that's OK." explained the boy. "I don't have to see it. I know it's up there. I can feel it tugging at the string." The baby, the minister said, would always be tugging at his parents' hearts. They would know he was there, with God, waiting for them.

I thought about Grandma Holt's funeral and wondered about the difference of lives. One can last ninety-six years, another is measured in hours. Both are complete. Both people share forever in God's life, tugging on the heart strings of those left behind.

~

Whether a life lasts for ninety-six years or an hour, everyone is part of the Incarnation. A long life brings God to others in ways we cannot see. The infant who lived for an hour outside his mother's womb had lived for nine months within. Those months were a time of preparation. His presence helped open his parents' hearts. His life gave them the opportunity to say "yes" to God, willing to place the needs of another above their own.

We all bring God's touch to the earth. God lives in us, and we share Jesus' mission to redeem the world. Whether it takes us decades or hours, we have a part in bringing the mystery of Incarnation to completeness.

ENDINGS AND BEGINNINGS

*Can a mother forget her infant, or be without tenderness
for the child of her womb? Even should she forget,
I will never forget you.*
Isaiah 49:15

Jolaine walked slowly back to the house after putting her youngest child on the bus for his first day of school. She had been up early and made a special breakfast. That was tradition. The older two were expecting it. Nicholas had been surprised. Worries about the day ahead had pushed breakfast from his mind.

As she walked in the back door, smells of bacon and syrup-smothered pancakes still hung in the air. The house was quiet. No little ones greeted her, begging for a share of the sweet breakfast. No one needed a story or a diaper changed. Everyone was in school!

A tear trickled down Jolaine's face as she poured a cup of coffee and pushed dishes away to make a space at the table. She sat down. It was the quiet she'd longed for so many times in the past. Why didn't it feel wonderful and freeing like she had imagined?

She remembered times when she couldn't even go to the bathroom without a toddler walking in and wanting to sit on her lap. What she would have given then for a few hours by herself! "Someday they'll all be in school," she had told herself. "Then I'll have a few minutes of peace."

That someday was now, and as much as she hated to admit it, it loomed long and empty before her. She'd miss Nicholas' questions, Sophia's silly jokes, and Michael's cars and trucks all over the house.

"I'm being foolish," she told herself. "It's only seven hours. Then they'll be home and it will be noisy again."

Still, it was the end of a chapter in her life. She would never again have her children toddling around the house, interrupting phone conversations and asking for stories. She wouldn't have a warm, blanket-wrapped little one to rock slowly after the others had gone.

Jolaine knew it was a beginning, too. New experiences, new challenges, new friends. But at the moment her tears were marking an end.

~

Today when at last I have time to myself, I'm not sure I want it. Thoughts of my children fill my head. I remember them little. I imagine them at school and I want to gather them up again and keep them close and safe.

Mary, mother of Jesus, you knew the joys and trials of having a young one around the house. I wonder if you ever tired of answering questions or washing soiled clothes. Was it difficult to watch Jesus grow and spend more of his time away from you and your house, where you could watch and protect him? Please, ask your son to keep my little ones in his care as they venture out into the world.

A PRAYER OF TEARS

❧

At the sight of her tears, and those of the Jews who
had come with her, Jesus was greatly distressed, and
with a profound sigh he said, "Where have you put
him?" They said, "Lord, come and see." Jesus wept.
John 11:35

"Grandma! Wanna see my gerbil?"

Carefully, Kathryn carried her new pet from her bedroom down the stairs and into the living room. Her grandma looked at the tiny, black gerbil.

"Ohh, it's so cute. Look at those shiny eyes. You know, when I was little, I had white mice."

She held the gerbil and admired it while Kathryn looked on proudly. Her sister had two gerbils. Her brother had a cat. Now, Kathryn had come of age. She, too, was old enough to care for an animal.

The gerbil was returned to the cage in the bedroom, but Kathryn went back upstairs to retrieve it when Grandpa arrived.

"Grandpa! I have a surprise for you!" she called.

I listened from the kitchen, waiting to hear my father's reaction to the new addition. Instead, I heard a little cry and then the thump, thump, thump of a child rolling down a flight of steps.

Before she had hit bottom, the family was there. Mom scooped Kathryn up in her arms. Dad checked to make sure she wasn't hurt.

Between sobs, Kathryn cried "My gerbil! My gerbil! I held on to him tight, so he wouldn't fall."

"Let me have him, honey," I said, and slowly opened her hand. The little animal lay limp, a black ball of fur.

97

"He's dead," her sister quietly observed. Kathryn screamed, laid her head on grandma's shoulder and sobbed. The three children carried the gerbil to the back yard. Holding it, they sat together and cried. Watching, I choked back tears myself.

The day before, I had taken her to the library to pick a gerbil from their prolific pair's newest litter. When we arrived, Kathryn carefully placed a tiny black one in a shoe box and cradled it in her lap as we drove home.

For one day she held it, fed it sunflower seeds, and smiled all the time. Now she buried the gerbil under the pine trees and marked the grave with a stick.

Trying to ease the hurt of the moment, Kathryn's grandma and I took her to a pet store to buy a new gerbil.

"I want a black one just like Flint," she said.

There were no black gerbils. Halfheartedly, she settled for a cinnamon-colored one.

A few days later I read an article about resisting the temptation to replace a pet as soon as it dies. Children need to grieve, the article said. A new pet never replaces the lost one. A child needs time to accept another.

I sighed as I read it. I remembered the children, sitting together, holding the dead gerbil, tears streaming down their faces. They had been grieving. Well-intentioned as we were, the adults did not understand their need.

A week later while we were feeding the new gerbil, Kathryn's eyes filled with tears.

"I miss Flint."

"Me too."

"Did you love her, Mom?"

"Yes. She was soft and shiny. I liked how she curled up and rested in my hand."

"Why didn't you cry, then? You know, when she died, you didn't cry."

"I wanted to, but I thought if I did you'd feel worse."

Kathryn crawled into my lap.

"I thought you didn't care."

We sat together on her bedroom floor and cried. She cried for her lost gerbil and the ache still left in her heart. I cried for Kathryn, for the little gerbil, and for all of us, who try to do our best with life's ups and downs, but often fall short.

~

Tears are a prayer of the heart that flow when words cannot carry the emotion. An act of intimacy, sharing tears binds us together when we experience deep feeling. How comforting to know that we have a God who desires intimacy with us, who shares in our suffering. When I am powerless in the grip of agony and sorrow, I will try to remember that moment with Kathryn. Just as my actions were a mystery to her, God's vision and plan are not my own. As I longed to comfort her, God longs to comfort me. The Holy One may not change events in my life in a way that I can understand, but he will cry with me.

PRESENCE

❧

When we are unable, God is able; when we feel
insufficient, God is always sufficient; when we are
filled with fear, God is always near.²
William Arthur Ward

Sheila, a friend from high school days, was expecting. She'd recently moved to Georgia, so when I wanted to know if the baby had arrived, I called her mother, who lives close by. Sheila had said her mom was suffering from the beginnings of Alzheimer's disease, but I hadn't noticed any symptoms when I talked with her a few months before. I decided to call. Sheila's mother answered the phone.

"Hello, Mrs. Benton?"

"Yes."

"This is Mary Holt, van Balen Holt. Sheila's friend."

"Oh, Mary. It's so good to hear your voice, dear. Bill, it's Mary. You remember..."

We talked for a minute or two. She seemed fine. "I called for Sheila's number, and to find out if she's had her baby yet."

"Her baby? Ummm. I think she did. Yes, yes, she did. It's a..." Pause. "It's a boy. They named him..." Pause. "Just a minute, honey."

She put her hand over the phone, but I could hear her asking her husband about the baby.

"Yes, yes," she said. "They named him Christopher."

"That's wonderful! How old is he?"

"Let's see... he was... Bill! How old is Christopher now? Three weeks? He's three weeks, Mary."

When I asked for her new phone number, Mrs. Benton began

100

rustling through some papers. Was she looking up the number? Trying to remember? The wait became long and uncomfortable. "Here it is! 479... 6... no... 9..."

She became agitated as she tried again and again to get it right.

"4769... 6... You'd better talk to Bill, honey. So nice hearing from you. Do call Sheila. She'd love it." Mr. Benton got on the phone and gave me the number. We exchanged a few pleasantries and hung up.

I went to the dining room table. The bottom dropped out of my stomach. Mrs. Benton couldn't remember her grandson's name or when he was born. She couldn't read numbers. This person I knew was trying to hang on, but slowly, she was slipping away.

~

My friend's mother is losing what keeps us anchored to society and the world. Memories, language, concepts are deserting her, frustrating attempts to connect with life around her. It grows worse. Her family and friends experience the loss of someone they love, even while her body is still very much alive.

Watching her struggle with this disease is frightening. It makes me wonder about the meaning and worth of life when what we usually associate with it is gone.

"Where is Jesus in all this?" Sheila asked one day. I don't know. Words and memories are gone, but presence remains. Mrs. Benton can feel an arm around her and a kiss on the cheek. Even on the day when her mother cannot remember who she is, Sheila will be present to care for her. She will sit with her mother because she loves her.

Is that where you are, Lord? You are God-with-us at the kitchen table, in the nursing home, when we remember and when we don't. You are Presence. When Mrs. Benton can no longer hold on to anything; while Sheila sees her mother passing from her life before she is physically gone; you are holding on to them both.

DIVINE JOY

❧

*We shall enter into a great sea of divine and eternal joy, which
will fill us within and without, and surround us on all sides.*[3]
Robert Bellarmine

My elderly aunt, Elvira, struggled for a year and a half
against recurring strokes. With valiant effort she battled
back after each one, regaining some faculties of speech and
mobility. Finally she could fight no more. She died at the age of
seventy-nine. We went to the funeral in Pennsylvania.

It was my children's first experience with death and the rituals
that surround it. I hoped I would find words to answer questions sure to come; words that would help them experience not
only the sadness of separation, but also the mystery and hope of
resurrection.

After a three-hour drive, we arrived at the funeral home. The
questions came, especially from the youngest. "It doesn't look
like Aunt Elvira," she said, peering cautiously into the casket.

I studied Elvira's face. It looked peaceful, but the spirit that
animated her body was gone.

"Well, it isn't Aunt Elvira any more," I answered. "It's just her
earth-body. She doesn't need it anymore. She's in heaven with
Jesus now."

"She is?"

"Mm-hmm."

"Oh." Pause. "Is she happy? Is she smiling right now?"

I tried to imagine where Aunt Elvira was. What would it be
like to make the passage from this life, through death, to new life,
letting go of everything we know? My aunt had done it. That

gave me hope.

"I'm sure she is."

"Oh, good!"

We found a seat and began visiting with family. For a while the children were interested to know how they were all related. After trying to keep confusing family ties straight, we decided to call just about everyone cousins. I smiled. Aunt Elvira would have loved it. She kept track of our family that stretched across the ocean, then across the country, writing a book that chronicled its history from 1700.

Early the following morning, we gathered in the funeral home for the last time.

"Why does she have a rosary in her hand?"

I remembered seeing the rosary entwined in Elvira's hands or laying on the end table when she visited my parents.

"She was a lady of great faith. She loved Jesus and Mary and Joseph. She said the rosary often."

"Really? She's happy now, we just can't see her, right?"

"Right."

"What makes her happy in heaven? Can she jump and run again and laugh with her new body in heaven?"

I wondered what heaven is like. Many images came to mind: The joyous reunion of the children with their parents in C.S. Lewis' *The Chronicles of Narnia*; a friend whose deep sense of peace and joy after a near-death experience left her with a renewed confidence in the afterlife; angels and robed figures from childhood school days. But all I was really sure of was that God made us to be with him, to be happy.

"She loves Jesus so much, she's happy just being with him. Besides, Jesus loves her so much he wants her to be happier than ever. Whatever she needs to be that happy, he'll make sure she has it."

My daughter squeezed my hand and smiled. We sat down. I had done all right.

~

I couldn't tell my daughter what heaven would be like or how we'll look when we get there. She didn't seem to mind the lack of specifics. God loves us. He will hold onto us when we are unable to hold on to anything, even our own lives. He made us to be happy. That was all she needed to know. It is enough for me, too.

THE NEW JOB

My Lord God, I have no idea where I am going. I do not see the road ahead of me. I cannot know for certain where it will end. Nor do I really know myself, and the fact that I think that I am following your will does not mean that I am actually doing so. But I believe that the desire to please you does in fact please you.[4]
Thomas Merton

As I got ready to go to work outside my home for the first time in seventeen years, I was nervous. The job was part-time, an elementary school resource teacher. It had been a long time since I'd had responsibilities like these. I wasn't used to getting up early and dressing in anything other than jeans and a sweater. My wardrobe had become meager and monotonous over the years. I looked in the mirror. The denim skirt and blazer would do.

As I fixed breakfast and packed lunches, I felt a pang of guilt. I wouldn't be home all day. What if one of the children got sick, or needed something? I checked the refrigerator. The meatloaf I had made the day before was ready to be put in the oven but I didn't kid myself. I knew I'd soon be joining the other working moms in line at the grocery store, buying deli-pizzas or roasted chicken after a long day on the job.

The children got off for school on time. Before she left, the youngest asked me again if I would be home when she got there. Guilt again. I would, but not always. I hadn't taught for seventeen years but I still remembered how involved I got. Despite good intentions of leaving on time each day, I would often be staying late to work on projects or look through papers. I gave her an extra hug.

105

"Pray for me honey. I'll pray for you. We'll do fine."

She smiled and walked to the bus stop.

I was reluctant to change our familiar family patterns. The job was something I like to do. It would be a way to serve others with the gifts I've been given. It would bring in a little extra money. Still, I wondered if I was doing the right thing.

"We'll do fine," I repeated to myself as I packed up my briefcase, walked outside, and locked the door. "We'll do fine, but it will never be quite the same again."

~

Lord, my most important call is to be wife and mother. I wonder if I will be able to add an outside job to my schedule and still be able to do the things that keep our home running smoothly and our family close. Time to be present to her family is one of a mother's gifts to them. It takes time to listen, to understand, to support, to celebrate, to pray. Will I still be able to do those things well?

Help me and my family, Lord. Give me the heart to try, but not to be seduced by this consumer culture's claim that money, job, and status are where our identity lies. My identity rests in you. May I discern if this job also is your will for me now. If it is not, give me the courage to let it go.

A TOOL IN THE ARTIST'S HANDS

*Yet, O Lord, you are our father, we are the clay and
you the potter: we are all the work of your hands.*
Isaiah 64:7

"My son is getting married," Julie told herself as she sorted through his clothes still left at home. She sat on the edge of his empty bed and stared into the open closet. In the corner she saw a beat-up cardboard box filled with airplane models and construction toys: remnants of childhood with which he'd been unwilling to part. Julie smiled, remembering the dark-haired toddler who used to run through the house, scattering small cars and trucks in his wake.

Six years ago, when Larry was a high school senior, she was ready to let him go. His need for independence was showing. He had been less interested in family rules and parental authority and more eager to try life on his own. It wasn't easy, but she and her husband had encouraged him to try.

Julie smiled again, remembering how they had packed their car with everything from clothes and a bicycle to stereo equipment and a small refrigerator.

The first month was the worst. Julie worried and prayed constantly. He was such a late sleeper. How would he ever get himself up for early classes? How would he manage his own laundry? The campus sprawled over many city blocks. The dorms were co-ed. She had wondered if Larry would go to church. Would he be able to avoid the temptations of drugs, alcohol, and sex so freely available? After sleepless nights, conversations with her husband, and much prayer, Julie knew she needed to trust her son to God. In the end, Larry did well. She did, too.

Now, Larry was getting married. Julie hardly knew the girl. "That happens when your kids go away to school," she thought. As she picked up the things Larry had asked her to send, she wondered and worried again.

"Will this marriage last? There's so much working against marriage these days. Are they right for each other? Their backgrounds are different. Will they have the faith to get them through, the faith that had sustained us through some rough times?"

The wedding will be in a park, a civil ceremony. It was not the wedding she'd imagined in her daydreams.

Julie put the last shirt in the box. Then, as an afterthought, she took a photo off the wall and slid it between the folded clothes. It was of the whole family on a camping trip. Julie thought it might keep him close to them; those memories, those seeds of love and faith planted years ago. Julie had to trust them now. She would welcome her daughter-in-law with love and warmth into the family. She would believe their marriage would last, and be there to help. She would pray. After all, they were God's children too. He wasn't finished with any of them yet.

~

Trusting our children to God is difficult. When they grow into adulthood and go out into the world on their own, we wonder if we have done a good job parenting. Have we given them what they will need? Have we held on too much, too little? Have we nurtured their faith? Respecting their decisions and allowing them to make their own mistakes takes tremendous trust in them, in ourselves, and in God.

There is a story told about Michaelangelo and his sculpting. When he worked, he wasn't chipping a figure from his own imagination out of the marble. He thought the form already existed. He could see it, already complete, trapped inside the block of stone. He chipped away the marble to set it free.

Holy One, who made us all, you alone can see the complete person you have made each of us to be. You know my children. I see only a small part of the creation they are. I am the chisel, not the artist. You have used me in many ways as I mother my children. Now, you have put me down for a while. There are other tools, other people, places, and events that you will use to set them free, these marvelous people, made in your own image.

"LITTLE DEATHS"

∾

What we call the beginning is often an end.
And to make an end is to make a beginning.
The end is where we start from.[5]
T.S. Eliot

One fall we hired a contractor to dry out our basement. I was sick with bronchitis, and unable to watch the work in progress. It included digging around the foundation to lay drainage tiles and waterproof the exposed block walls.

After recovering, I went outside with my husband to see what had been done. Immediately, I noticed the absence of my favorite rock. Carried home from the Black Hills of South Dakota, it was a mix of milky white quartz and silver mica. When sunlight hit it in the mornings, the quartz seemed to glow from within. The mica reflected bright light back to the sky like a mirror. It always reminded me of prayer near Harney Peak, and Black Elk, the Oglala holy man whose book had filled me with longing to go to the holy land of the Lakota.

The rock had survived fifteen years and six moves. After the workers left, it was buried eighteen inches underground somewhere around the house. At first, I was angry that no one had thought to move it to safety. I mourned its loss. Eventually, I let it go. The striking rock had turned my heart to the God of all people. But the connection with the mystery and prayer of the Black Hills was within me, not dependent on the rock. I did not need to hold on.

Life is full of "little deaths." I remember one night in my early college days sitting alone after an evening with a male friend. I felt very much in love with him. However, our relationship would never culminate in marriage. Pain and longing to hold on to some false hope filled my heart. I knew I had to let it go. "It's one more death," I told myself. "One more chance to practice letting go." I hated it, but I embraced it and prayed God was holding on to me.

~

Lord, our final, physical death comes after we have had many occasions to practice letting go. "Little deaths" are part of our lives from their beginnings: having to share with other children; a best friend choosing other companions in junior high; a college scholarship not coming through; the job we want going to someone else; the long-awaited weekend with our spouse canceled when a child becomes ill; choosing the less attractive of two job offers because it is not as disruptive to family life; poor health requiring a change in lifestyle.

Like a mother standing beneath her child hanging from a tree branch, but afraid to let go, you are with us whispering "Let go, let go. Don't be afraid. I've got you."

Trusting that voice is difficult, but it become easier with practice. Thank you Lord, for the "little deaths" you have put in my life. Help me embrace them and see them as the gift they are: opportunities to grow in the certainty of faith I will need when the time of physical death arrives.

PART FIVE

WONDER

In *One Small Blue Bead,* by Byrd Baylor Schweitzer, a blue bead in the desert sand leads the narrator to tell of a young boy and an old man. Both are dreamers and members of a prehistoric clan of cave dwellers who believe themselves to be unique in the world. Listening to men talk, Boy hears the old man share an astounding thought: Somewhere, others like themselves exist. He wants to find them.

"But Boy was filled with wonder./ This new thought was a thunder/ In his mind."

Despite the fear and ridicule of others, Boy offers to do the work of two so the old man will be free to follow his heart's desire. "I think that there is something/ That just tells a man to go/ In search of people who may not be,/ In search of places he may not see./ Still he has to search./ That's clear to me."[1]

Sometimes in our fast-paced, modern world, we hunger for such a sense of wonder. Where in our lives do we find something to call it forth? Media speaks in hyperbole. Unusual or bizarre happenings are fashioned into stories for national consumption. We are flooded with amazing things everyday. Communication bounces off satellites and flows electronically over the Internet. Instantaneously, we can be in touch with people and places around the world, under the sea, or out in space. We have left footprints and trash on the moon. Some speculate that soon parents will be able to select a child trait by trait. No surprises. We are jaded by the surfeit of scientific and technological advances.

I remember sitting with the rest of my fifth grade class on the day Alan Shepard made his arc through space. The cloth-covered intercom, nestled between crucifix and blackboard, broadcast radio coverage of the event. Led by our teacher—a nun who probably witnessed the transition from horse to horseless buggies and who viewed this new event with skepticism and trepidation—we prayed the rosary from liftoff to splashdown. Now, I can't keep track of shuttle missions.

We cannot count on extraordinary events to elicit a sense of wonder. Neither can we blame science and technology for banishing mystery from our lives. Indeed, science gives us many opportunities to ponder the spiritual. No, we filter out mystery from life ourselves with our perception of the reality around us.

How can Mother Teresa see the face of Jesus when everyone else sees a sick beggar? How can a photographer shoot two rolls of film on upturned tree roots that clog the creek? What moved the old man in *One Small Blue Bead* to see the possibility of unseen caves sheltering unknown people when others saw only endless, empty landscape?

The difference is in perception. Wonderment arises from how we experience reality, not from what the reality is. Life is crammed with things that can be thunder in our minds and in our souls. Something as ordinary as a feather or stone on our path; something as small as an atom or the forces that bind it together; something as huge as the ocean or the star-studded sky; something as close as the face of our spouse or as far away as a distant galaxy; when seen as a reflection of God's Presence with us, they can move us to reverent awe before the Creator.

To be filled with a sense of wonder, we must cultivate the contemplative in us. Looking deeply, experiencing deeply, we realize we are in the presence of God. That knowing fills us with awe. Then, like the boy in the story, we will be filled with wonder, a thunder in our minds.

THE MEASURE OF A LIFE

*Lord, make me like crystal that your light
may shine through me.*[2]
Katherine Mansfield

Hoping to learn more about the artist and her work, I walked up narrow steps to the small gallery. Roselle Davenport's paintings hung like windows on the white walls; windows to life experiences, distilled through her soul and brush. After a brief look around, I picked a seat in the neatly arranged rows and waited for the lecture to begin.

Her slight frame resting in a tall director's chair, Roselle faced the gathering crowd. Except for a colorful scarf, she was dressed entirely in black. A hat covered her head, its soft fur brushing her eyebrows. Wrapped in a long coat, she looked pale. And vulnerable. I studied her graceful hands. They were old. Her fingers were long and delicate. How many years had they held pencil and brush? Having been ill, she waited for her artist son, Anthony, to begin the lecture she had intended to deliver herself: "The Creative Journey."

Starting with her early portraits, he moved through the years and the places: New York, Hawaii, Southern France. He guided us through subject matter and style.

Watching the slides and the artist sitting before me, I was drawn into her journey. The creative journey and the spiritual journey are one. To experience her paintings was to encounter a bit of the Spirit that dwells in all life. Her images were piercingly honest. An attempt to communicate the essence of her experience, they were without addition or aggrandizement; true experience of a moment requires none. Roselle Davenport's paintings grew out of her prayer. They *were* prayer. Some were clear, like unblemished glass. For a moment they allowed me to be where she had been, experiencing some smattering of the soul of life that she had known.

I spoke briefly with Roselle after the lecture before wandering through the gallery contemplating her work. All art that celebrates life is "sacred." It is a dim reflection of God's splendor that stirs the spirit and fills it with joy. This work humbled me. I was in the presence of the Holy One and one who has labored faithfully to share her vision. The evening was awash in prayer: the artist's mingling with my own.

~

The artist did not "capture" her experience of life on the canvasses for others to view dispassionately. What she created allowed the essence of her experience to flow, to live, to engage the one who sees. She had given us a window to pass into other times and places.

Lord, most mothers do not have walls of paintings or shelves of books to chronicle their journeys. But, like the artist, we try to be honest and faithful to our call. We share our own experiences of God with our families. We become windows that allow the bit of God we know to shine into the world and into the lives of those we love.

Moments of
Awakening

*Take from me, good Lord, this lukewarm fashion, or
rather cold manner of meditation and this dullness in
praying to you. And give me warmth, delight
and life in thinking about you.[3]*
Thomas More

A flood of sound and soul spilled into the quiet afternoon as
the wooden church door opened. Magnificent sounds of the
pipe organ washed over me. Swelling chords and pulsating bass
vibrated the Gothic stone arches. Someone was playing; not practicing for Sunday Mass, but playing from the heart. My step
slowed. I stopped and lit a candle but resisted the temptation to
sit quietly and listen. I had come for the Eucharist to bring to a
homebound parishioner.

Reverently, I climbed the steps to the altar and placed the
Eucharist in a small, gold pyx. The intense crescendo of music
arrested my step. I looked up at the choir loft and watched the
organist. The player and the music were one. I imagined the
notes being pulled from the depth of his heart: prayer beyond
words, rushing out in glorious completeness, filling the building.
One moment it was triumphant, the next, wrung with the groan-
ing St. Paul attributes to all creation.

I felt my own heart stir. Longing to pray, to let the slumbering
desire for oneness with life and God waken within me, I stood
still and listened. The music had roused something deep inside. It

117

felt good. It felt like a full draught of fresh autumn air, crammed with scents familiar, yet unrecognized; smells that stir memories buried, but ready to break into consciousness.

I thought about waiting a while. The music, the building, and the flickering candles blended into a meditative stillness. It offered my heart the needed space to remember some of the mystery and promise God had placed there. But I had a long list of errands and was unable to let them go. I left.

~

Scraping against the rough surfaces of life has dulled the edge of my prayer. Once able to cut cleanly through preoccupations of the day to quiet moments of contemplation, I now struggle to get in touch with my spiritual self. Life goes on. I become preoccupied with its tasks. In the process, longings and gifts of the heart can be pushed deep within to a place I seldom go. What must I do to feel intensely again? To experience your presence? To let the prayer in my heart rise to my lips?

Thank you Lord, for breaking into the routine of my life through the inspirited music. Help me recognize moments of awakening, making time for them when they come.

WHAT FEET HAVE WALKED THESE PATHS?

❧

*... for what is one man that he should make much of
his winters, even when they bend him like a heavy snow?
So many other men have lived and shall live that
story, to be grass upon the hills.*[4]
Black Elk

In the company of our daughter's fifth- and sixth-grade classes, my husband and I spent hours viewing a Hopewell Indian mound and exploring caves. We squeezed through mazes of rock and still-growing stalactites. I laid my hand on a stalagmite thousands of years old and thought about those who had gone before us, locked away now in the silence of prehistory.

I wondered whose ancient hands had also rested on that same spot. How did those people speak to one another? What did they think of when they looked up at the star-studded sky? How did they understand the mysteries of the world? How did they worship? They lived, raised children, and died. God knew them as he knows me.

Afternoon sun sparkled off high cliff walls, wet with groundwater. A small spring gurgled out of rocks near my feet. Had this been a resting place? Was it once a place where women gathered to collect water for their families?

Other feet had walked these paths, other eyes had seen the beauty of these caves. I thought these things as we climbed onto the bus but was jolted back into the present by thirty-four twentieth-century students.

119

~

Visiting places that bear the mark of ancient human hands is humbling. It connects me with a truth I know, but often do not remember: We are but one small contribution to the reality of creation. I am important because I can reflect some part of the Creator into time and space. I am important because I am loved by that One. Still, I am only one. Countless others, loved as myself, have tread this earth.

"...AND TOUCH THE FACE OF GOD..."

*Seeing this has to change a man, has to make a man
appreciate the creation of God and the love of God.[5]*
James Irwin

It's an unorthodox prayerbook: no hymns, psalms, or familiar prayers. No pictures of Jesus, saints, or stained glass windows. It is written by scientists from many countries. They are people of many faiths and of no particular faiths. Orbiting the earth at least once is the common experience that binds them together. Their words, and their photographs of the earth from space, are the source of my reflections.

I can spend hours contemplating the pages of *The Home Planet.* Color, texture, and perspective pull me away from my usual vantage point. Creation and my place in it looks different from one thousand miles up, yet hauntingly the same. Subtle shades of brown, gray, and rose meet and blend in a view of Iran and the Zagros mountains taken from Challenger 6 in October, 1984. I have seen those colors, those patterns before: a sandstone slice from Colorado; a thin scale of bark; a rock from Hocking Hills. Tennyson said that if he could understand the tiny flower, root and all, he would understand all. Was he experiencing the sense of Wholeness in which all things sink their roots and have their being?

Some photographs in the book, exquisite in design and color, elicit a gasp of recognition from my soul. Color and shape in juxtaposition speak an ancient, deep language my spirit understands. Intellect steps aside and watches the movement toward wholeness that I feel but cannot tell.

The Great Himalayas are carved in rich browns. White ferns of snow drape along the ridges and feather the crevices. The same pattern, in green, covers woodland floors when fiddlehead, maidenhair, and Christmas ferns spread their fronds. Ice crystals on loose-fitting storm doors and windows echo the design.

~

All is one. The space travelers' words speak what my heart knows. Oneness embraces all. It binds all creation from the limits of space to the tiniest particle. It places us in the Presence of God, from whose hand it flows.

A RENEWED SPIRIT

*The Lord is my shepherd; I shall not want. He maketh me
to lie down in green pastures: he leadeth me beside
the still waters. He restoreth my soul.*
Psalm 23:1-3 KJV

I call it our "wonder basket." Hand made in South Carolina, it
was painstakingly fashioned from bundles of sweet grass bound
together with strips of palmetto. I can still smell the pungent
aroma of sweet grass when I put my nose close to it, or rinse it
with cool water. The oval basket is four inches deep and sits on top
of the dining room buffet. It holds family treasures. Some days I
take a break from my routine and poke through its contents.

What a diverse accumulation it is. A small plastic box is filled
with light gray ash from the eruption of Mt. St. Helens. You can
see each grain through the magnifier lid. Imagine the force that
could blow off the top of a mountain! It scattered ash like snow
that was plowed and piled along the roads. The basket holds a
calico scallop shell I found at the beach. Fossils, rocks, and shells
from vacations and walks in the woods are tumbled together.
Looking further I see mica from Colorado, a turkey feather, a
green iridescent feather one of the children found somewhere, a
turtle shell, a puff ball, and an old coin found with a metal detec-
tor. A few magnifying glasses and a kaleidoscope are tucked in to
afford a closer or different look.

Sometimes the basket gets lost in the clutter and busyness of
family life. When rediscovered, it never disappoints. No matter
how jaded I feel, a few minutes of sifting through the basket and
its treasures rekindles my ability to wonder.

~

We are like a wonder basket, filled with our life's accumulation of memories, thoughts, and feelings. They speak of God's Presence with us. Like the basket on my buffet, those things that remind us of God get buried under concerns and work of day-to-day life. Sometimes when we feel abandoned or worn down by life's demands, it is good to sit quietly, and sift through the memories we have stored within. Given time, they turn our minds and hearts again to God. They allow us to be in awe of the One who made all things and yet has chosen to be with us. Our spirits are renewed.

PERCEPTION VS. REALITY

*Mach's principle that the element of wonder never lies in
the phenomenon, but always in the person observing.*[6]
P. Fitzgerald

Webster states that "perception" is consciousness as well as a capacity for understanding. A conversation with my teenage son made me ponder the defining power of perception in our lives. We were driving through the countryside along a state route when a motorcycle passed us.

"Did you see that?" Josh asked as it sped away.

"What? The motorcycle? Yes, I saw it."

He then went on to describe in detail the type of engine it had and other attributes that were a mystery to me.

"How can you tell all that? We only saw it for a few seconds."

"It had four exhaust pipes and . . ."

His explanation made no sense to me. I relegate motorcycles to a whole class of objects I will never know much about. Two wheels, dangerous, fast. That is my limited perception of "motorcycleness." However, I am much better at birds. Further along on our ride I spotted a bird flying up from the grassy meadow along the road.

"Did you see that?" I asked.

"What? The bird? Yes, I saw it."

I proceeded to describe the meadowlark, its yellow breast marked with a black "V," its alternating pattern of short wing beats and then a glide. I looked over at my son. He was reading. His understanding of birds was right up there with my consciousness of motorcycles. That is all right. We cannot be equally aware of everything. Our experience of life needs to be filtered through perceptions or we would be on overload. Still, I thought about how limiting perceptions can be and wondered how they might be expanded.

In her book *Plain and Simple*, Sue Bender reflects on her time living with the Amish and how it affected her. It broadened her perception of some "housework": "Stripped down, pared down, the house came alive. Nothing changed and everything changed. Nothing special and everything special. Taking care of my home was no longer a chore. Like a Zen monk raking the white pebbles at the temple, I spent seven minutes each morning sweeping the black floor. A meditation."[7]

What had changed was her perception of the work she was doing, and that changed everything. Our capacity to understand and perceive the countless nuances and layers of meaning in our lives determines how we experience life. I wonder how many I have missed altogether, like motorcycles.

~

How have I limited my experience of God by what I expect God to be? For those who believe God is interested and active in the lives of ordinary people, seeing his hand in their lives will be possible. For those who believe God is distant and impersonal, too "cosmic" to be involved with human life, God's hand will be more difficult to see.

Jesus, open my mind and heart to new understandings. Help me sense more of the mystery and wonder of life. Free me from my established ways of viewing the world that limit my experience of your Presence.

GOD'S GLORY

～

Great is God our Lord. Great is his power, and there
is no end to his wisdom. Praise him you heavens.
Glorify him sun and moon and you planets, for out
of him, through him, and in him are all things, every
perception and every knowledge.[8]

Johannes Kepler,
German astronomer 1571-1630

My son and I sat on the couch as in a pew. The PBS special
Creation of the Universe was our liturgy. Scientists articulating theories, computer-generated images, and breathtaking photography processed across the screen. Pulling me deeper into the spell, the music swelled and softened like an organ. This science does not diminish mystery.

Peeling back layer after layer of pollen blossoms, computer images pulled us into a sub-atomic world. Next we observed nuclear forces and saw how they might combine, bringing us closer to a unified theory. A Z-particle bent gracefully in its middle like a thin wire with spheres at each end. Each bowing toward the other, the spheres arched smoothly until they touched. The decaying particle transformed into a photon shooting out like a comet. Decaying itself, the photon became two weak bosons. They recombined to form a Z-particle. The dance of energy goes on.

From the sub-atomic world, we were catapulted into the far reaches of the universe. I gazed into the primeval past. Clouds of helium and hydrogen swirled. Matter crystallized from the cooling soup: stars lit the darkness; planets coalesced. Genesis. Is that where, for a brief moment, everything was one? Is that where the elusive unified theory hides? Is that God's creating moment?

Powerful intellects stretch and groan to understand what remains unknowable to creaturely minds. Still, they search. They are looking for the simple, beautiful idea that is the key to the why of the universe.

We listened and wondered and stretched our minds as far as they could go. When the special ended, I turned off the TV. We sat in silence. With Galileo, Kepler, and Einstein, I bent my knees and bowed my head. The evidence of God's glory spins through space-time and dances in the atoms that make up my body.

~

Like sitting at the ocean's edge, surrounded by water and sand at every wave, I sat surrounded by mystery. The scientists' words invited my mind to soar. I relished the thought of ancient light illuminating present nights in a world of energy dancing within me.

Lord, thank you for a faith that does not fear new ideas or intellectual pursuits. Thank you for the gift great thinkers and scientists have to share. Thank you for this wondrous universe. All our efforts to understand its origin and unfolding are efforts to find you.

PART SIX

WAITING

A mother's life is filled with waiting. If we listen to our culture's cry, however, we won't find it a satisfying way to spend time. From fast food to instant money machines, the message is clear: waiting wastes time. The faster we can get one thing done, the more time we have to do something else. The assumption, of course, is that more is better.

Instant gratification is another antagonist in the waiting game. Promoted as a proper expectation, it denigrates waiting. If we don't have cash, charge it. At work, we like instant feedback. At home we like to see quick results after instructions: a clean bedroom, or a changed attitude. Even computers fall short. I admit to becoming impatient with mine after using a newer one at work. How slow my own was to respond to the typed commands! Six months after purchasing a new one, I am disappointed that it does not have CD-ROM! And even that has already been superseded by more technological wizardry. I will always want something new.

Yet deep within, there is an uncomfortableness with so much hurry. Hurry to do. Hurry to have. Perhaps it is a feminine wisdom that warns against this assault on waiting. Waiting is a necessary and integral part of woman's nature. There is no hurrying pregnancy. A woman quietly holds new life within to give it time to grow and become ready for birth. Nurturing children and relationships takes patience and time. Women (and the feminine wisdom within men) know this. There are times to be active and times to be still. There are times to anticipate, to linger, to pause. Seeing the results of her efforts is a pleasure often delayed. Sometimes they are never known with certainty. And yet, the contribution such love, patience, and nurturing make to our world is vital.

The world suffers for its sin of refusing to wait. When knowledge and technology become available, we proceed. We have rushed into dilemmas in many fields: medicine, arms, chemical research, technology. People and ideas that have been growing and germinating have been trod over in our hurry to get results. Who knows what gifts have been lost?

However, in a world that sorely needs the feminine gift of valuing process as much as product, women themselves have often forgotten this truth: waiting can be a time of grace. A time to remember that the God we seek is already with us. To be still is not to be wasting time. To be still is to open us up to receive. Time to anticipate, to prepare, to nurture is as important as what we anticipate, prepare for, and nourish. It is a gift to reclaim and to give.

OUT OF CONTROL

They who wait upon the Lord will renew their strength.
Isaiah 40:31

Pregnancy has never been as easy for me as it is for my sister. She glows when she is pregnant. I throw up. She gives birth at home and eats ice cream with her family around the kitchen table half an hour later. My milk won't come in.

Of my three pregnancies, the first was physically the easiest. Emotionally, it was most difficult. The transition into first-time motherhood is filled with strong emotions: fear and doubt as well as joy and anticipation.

Then came number two. All went well until the last four weeks. Excruciating back pain signaled the gymnast inside had changed position. Recovering from the Caesarean was slow.

"The third time will be the best," I told myself. Pedaling away on a borrowed exercise bicycle, I made a plan. Bouncing back would be easier with toned muscles and a healthy body.

The obstetrician tempered my enthusiasm. A sonogram revealed I had *placenta previa:* the placenta covered the cervix rather than attaching itself to the side of my uterus.

"It may change position somewhat as the pregnancy progresses," he said handing us soundwave "photos" of our baby. "It can cause problems later on: bleeding or rupturing. Good luck. I hope you can carry your baby to term."

The remark, meant to be encouraging, let doubt into my heart.

Months went by with no problems. I grew confident. Then, the spotting began. With prayer, rest, and help from family, the

131

weeks dragged by. My husband and I pulled out of commitments and skipped activities. After more serious bleeding, complete bedrest was prescribed. We moved in with my parents.

Meals were brought to me. My children came upstairs to "visit." My only exercise was walking to the bathroom. In long, quiet stretches of time alone, I began to feel sorry for myself. Nothing was going as planned. I wanted to be out of bed, taking care of my family. I wanted the baby to be born safely. I wanted to be in control again.

Tears rolled down my face. Slowly, I understood: I could not be in control again. I had *never* been in control. Not really.

~

Lord, so many people talk about women having the right to be in control of their own bodies. As if they could. We all are responsible for what we do with our bodies, but that is not the same as being in control.

Being in control is an illusion shouted at us from every corner of our culture: Do this and you will live long. Do this and you will increase your intelligence. Buy this and you will be happy. Wear this and you will be beautiful and sexy.

Waiting for our daughter, Kathryn, to be born helped me understand our dependence on you. I lay still, in bed, and bled anyway. I could do nothing to ensure the safety of the child within.

Lord, you called me to deeper trust, your whisper silencing the need to control. "Do not fear," you spoke in my heart. "I am God. The child is mine." Overcome by your grace, fear slipped away.

THE LINE

So the last shall be first, and the first shall be last.
Matthew 20:16

You know the dilemma: After loading your grocery cart, you approach the front of the store and scan the checkout lines. The challenge is to determine which one will move fastest. One has a new cashier. The one with no bagger is also out. Finally, you roll the cart behind a lady whose groceries are half checked through.

Then comes the familiar call: "Dan, I need a price check." That's just the beginning. The customer searches her purse for three coupons. When she finds them, two have expired. She's picked up the wrong size cereal for the third. A bagger is sent to make the exchange. The lady pays with an out-of-state check. She fumbles with a wallet that looks like a file cabinet to find her driver's license.

Whether in a grocery store, post office, or bank, I have a talent for picking the slowest line. Careful consideration and experience count for nothing. This is especially irritating when I am rushing home from work or squeezing the errand between two other commitments.

Sometimes, in those situations, I decide on one line and deliberately walk into a different one. Maybe I can outsmart myself. Not usually. When I'm in a hurry, the whole world slows down.

~

Lord, help me think about others instead of myself as I wait in line. Perhaps the older gentleman who draws out a conversation

133

with the cashier goes home to an empty house. The new cashier who is painfully slow may be unsure of herself, starting back to work after years at home with her family. Embarrassed by the cries of her toddler, a young mother would appreciate a kind smile and assurances that the same thing happened when my children were small.

What makes my schedule more important than the needs of others? Waiting in line is an opportunity to put others first.

A Visit to the ER

∾

*"Let the little children come to me; do not stop them.... "
Then he put his arms round them, laid his hands on
them and gave them his blessing.*
Mark 10:13-16

Waiting in the emergency room of a children's hospital puts my problems in perspective. When Kathryn fell and deeply cut her cheek, I knew she would need stitches. Rick and I piled the children into the car.

"Will it hurt?" Kathryn wanted to know.

The older two children, veterans themselves, reassured her. While they went through the procedure, step by step, I hoped the technician would do an exceptional job.

Emergency room personnel are trained to handle the most serious problems first. After checking Kathryn and recording necessary information, we were directed to the waiting room.

Large televisions beamed news and sitcoms from their place on the walls. Few watched. Most of us were absorbed in comforting our hurting children and keeping an eye on the restless ones who were brought along.

Kathryn drifted off to sleep in my arms. I observed others in the room. An assortment of children suffered cuts, sprains, and deep coughs. One woman cradled a girl who looked about eight years old. She was ashen gray and burning with fever. Solemnly bent over her, the mother's head rested on the child's chest, listening for each shallow breath.

"It's our third time this week," she confided in me.

They were quickly taken back to the examining room.

Occasionally a nurse would wheel a crib bed down the hall. Their tiny occupants looked fragile, hooked up to IVs and surrounded by folded blankets to keep them from rolling.

As time stretched on, I thought about the young people in the hospital I could not see, but knew were there: children battling cancer, losing a limb, seriously ill. I prayed for them and for their mothers.

Twice an ambulance siren pierced the walls. Children were wheeled in and through the automatic sliding doors. Were they victims of car accidents, street violence, abuse?

"Kathryn Holt?"

We stood up and followed the nurse.

~

All mothers want their children's lives to be perfect and unmarred by suffering, injury, and pain. Infants begin life innocent and full of promise. Then come injuries that cut their flesh and bruise their spirits.

The first hurts are especially difficult for us mothers. They are visible signs that even our precious children are vulnerable. No one is immune from suffering and pain. Children everywhere are learning to confront life's harsher side: illness, war, famine, violence, and often with great courage. As I sat in the waiting room, my prayer grew from one for Kathryn to one that included all children. I pleaded with the God who placed little ones on his knee. "Bless them all. Strengthen them. Heal the broken bodies and hearts of your beloved children."

WHAT REALLY MATTERS

It is always possible to be thankful for what is given, rather than complain about what is not given.[1]
Elisabeth Elliot

I cashed the paycheck and distributed the money among envelopes for savings, checking, groceries, gas, and allowances. After re-counting, I smiled. No mistake. This time we had more than usual to put aside for "extras."

"Mom! Hey, Mom!"

Thoughts of a quiet dinner for two at a local restaurant were interrupted by my daughter.

"Carol invited me to her birthday party Friday. Can I go? I know just what I want to get her."

"Sure," I said.

The next day, we went shopping. The gift Kathryn picked was more costly than usual, but I was feeling expansive. By mid-week, I was still hoping for dinner out with my husband. However, the fund for luxuries took another hit.

"Are my tetanus shots up to date?" our fourteen-year-old asked.

"Yes." I waited for details.

"Well, I just wondered. I mean, I cut my leg on a rusty nail when I climbed down the tree by the cabin. It's funny, I didn't see it when I climbed up."

I wasn't laughing. The drive to our pediatrician's office is a half an hour each way. I watched the needle on the gas gauge fall. There went the week's gas money.

"My jeans got ripped, too, Mom."

"Your good ones? The ones you wear to school?"

"Yes. I'm really sorry. Maybe we could stop at the mall on the way home. My other pair is getting small, too."

A few days later the car's muffler dropped off, and my husband stripped a plug while changing the oil. The romantic dinner out was downgraded to a carryout pizza. Even that became out of the question when our son needed supplies for metal shop and fees for the ACT application.

Soon I was carding gas and figuring out how to stretch the pantry contents until Friday. And, as usual, waiting for the next paycheck.

~

In college I was a '60s flower child. My studies offered little in the way of monetary return: social work, fine arts, anthropology. For those like myself, committed to service, creativity, and learning for the joy of it, pursuit of money was anathema! Beaded and bell-bottomed, we didn't socialize much with the groomed and button-downed types in more conventional courses of study.

Thirty years and a family later, my views about money have changed. A large house, nice vacations, and a reliable car no longer seem sure signs of misplaced values. I wouldn't object if the prize patrol showed up at my house.

Yet, as we stretch our budget from paycheck to paycheck, I remind myself that our real needs are being met. Many people have no paycheck. No home. No opportunities. In the global picture, we are doing very well.

What has been the path from ascetic college student to restless, middle-aged wife and mother? What sows seeds of discontent?

Lord, fill my heart with gratitude for the many blessings we have known. When counting pennies becomes disheartening, help me refocus on truly important matters, and be generous with what I have been given.

GENERATIONS

∾

Fix these words of mine in your hearts and minds...
teach them to your children...
Deuteronomy 11:18-19

The muffled sound of school bells floated into the street. Putting down my book, I turned to watch students pour out of the brick building. Cars lined the curb: parents waiting for sons and daughters. After months of this ritual, I was learning to match teens with cars as I waited for my son. Had the diversity of students been as great in my freshman class? Some students emerging into the afternoon sun could have passed for sixth-graders. Others had afternoon shadows and looked twenty. At forty-four, I have never looked as sophisticated as some of the girls: hair carefully yet casually coifed, make-up flawlessly applied. Occasionally, someone walked by who reminded me of myself thirty years ago: awkwardly trying to appear mature. I had worn knee socks and saddle shoes with my uniform jumper.

Giggles broke into my reverie. A group of girls were casting quick glances at a boy with blue hair who passed by. On our morning run, my son and I sometimes watch black-jacketed punkers hang out in a church parking lot near the school. Blue hair one day might be green, pink, or striped the next. Girls in my day had gotten in trouble for teasing theirs.

More students sauntered out of the building. I watched cheerleaders practice on the lawn. Recycled fashions of the sixties made me feel old: flannel shirts, hiking boots, even a few bell bottoms. Peace signs are no longer a protest. They are a fashion statement.

139

Finally, a familiar sweatshirt and blond head appeared in the crowd. I watched my son make his way to the car.

"Hi, Mom!" he said, flopping down on the seat next to mine.

"Hi, Bud. How was your day?"

~

Usually turbulent teenage years are made more difficult by a culture that offers no ethical moorings. Many young people have little guidance as they grow, change, and make decisions that will impact their lives for years to come.

Memories of my teen years are mixed. My generation struggled, as all do, on the way to adulthood. However, today's youth face special challenges. They experience pressures and dilemmas I never imagined.

While I scan the group of students, waiting for my own, I pray for them all. May God bless each one with people who will listen; who believe in them and challenge them; who care enough to look with them at the difficult questions. Lord, send people of faith and love into the lives of these students. Whether they have brown hair or green, wear flannel or black leather and silver chains; whether they look hard and old beyond their years, or young and bewildered, they are yours.

I pray for myself and for those of my generation. May we be generous with our time and love. May we be courageous in our example of faith. May we serve you in your children.

TIME FOR PRAYER

ও

*We can make our heart a prayer room into which we
can retire from time to time to converse with
him gently, humbly and lovingly.*[2]
Brother Lawrence

Worn down by life's hectic pace, I sometimes seek quiet and comfort in our old stone church. Neo-gothic in design, its vaulted ceiling, towering pillars, and cool, dim interior sweep me out of my twentieth-century lifestyle and into *karios*, God's own time. If only its power could be put in a bottle! I'd pull it out when I caught myself running to maintain a frenetic schedule. Or when demands of family, home, and work overwhelm. It would pull me back to my center.

Years ago, a friend shared some wisdom with me. A member of a contemplative order, she occasionally helped run errands for her community. She had a way of living in *karios* no matter where she was.

"When I knew I had a long wait for someone to pick me up, I just closed my eyes and began mental prayer. We have to get in three hours a day, you know. I couldn't let that time slip away. People wondered how I could be so patient. They didn't understand. I wasn't waiting. I was praying."

Few eyebrows would raise at the sight of a nun in habit, serenely sitting deep in prayer. When I try it, most people must assume I'm sleeping, or mentally reviewing the next few stops on my schedule. Both are likely to be true. Still, when I remember, I try to place myself in the quiet and comfort of God's time, even if only for a few minutes. When the schedule resumes, I am ready.

141

It's like emerging from our old stone church. Refreshed and peaceful, I resume my twentieth-century pace knowing all centuries rest in God.

~

I have a wasteful habit of using time spent waiting to worry over what I could be doing if I wasn't stuck in a line, a bank, a dentist's office, or a car. Mentally juggling work to be done with time available wastes the present moment.

Holy One, help me see waiting time as a gift. My work will be there when I get home or back to school. Moments when I can do nothing but wait are moments of grace. Since I can do nothing about the laundry, shopping, or a child's school project while caught in a traffic jam (no car phones for me!), or a doctor's office, I am free. Free to remember that the time I experience as constantly flowing forward is really existing in entirety in you. In the present moment, I meet you, and am refreshed.

WAITING UP

❧

Who of you by worrying can add a single hour to his life?
Since you cannot do this very little thing,
why do you worry about the rest?
Luke 12:25-26

She sat at the kitchen table, waiting for her teenage son to return from a post-basketball game party. Everyone else was in bed. She read and wrote a note to a friend. Worry kept intruding. What if he had an accident? What if "something" happened? After nodding off a few times, she brewed more coffee.

She watched the clock and fought sleep. Midnight. One. Two. Two-thirty. Anger began to overshadow concern. How could he be so inconsiderate? At least he could call. She went over her conversation with him before he left. Word by word, she remembered it all.

He was going to play in the game. Then, his friends were going over to Tom's house for a party. Hopefully, a celebration. Then he had asked....

A sheepish grin spread over her face. Then she laughed out loud, her anger and worry gone. How could she have forgotten? He had asked if he could spend the night. She had said yes.

〜

When my sisters and brothers and I were growing up, our mother stayed awake until we were safely home at night. Sometimes her presence was comforting. After an unhappy or confusing evening, I welcomed the sound of her voice. We could

143

talk. She was stability in my unpredictable world.

At other times I resented the "intrusion." "How foolish," I thought. "I'm practically an adult." I knew where I was and felt perfectly capable of taking care of myself. Even when she wasn't downstairs, I knew she was awake. The "click" of the small, bedside light going off gave her away.

Now my friends and I are doing the same thing. We wait. We pray for our children's safe return. Hoping we have taught them well, we are busy but aware of the clock. Only after the last child walks in does sleep come to stay.

Lord, I know you care for my children with a love deeper than my own. When my youngest asks me how that can be, I do not know. I cannot imagine a love deeper than my own. Yet it is true. They are your children.

Now is the time for them to accept more responsibility for their lives. They venture further from home. I must entrust them to you, I know. I try. Still, I stay awake until all are gathered back into our home, wrapped with the love you've given me to share.

THE BIOPSY

But I trusted in thee O Lord. I said, Thou art my God.
My times are in thy hands.
Psalm 31:14-15 KJV

Martha had scheduled the biopsy for early Friday morning so she could be home before school was over. She pulled on a sweater. Looking in on her children asleep in their beds, she wondered whether this day would change the rest of their lives. Despite the sweater, she shivered.

Her last mammogram had shown a white mass in her left breast.

"You should see your doctor, and schedule a biopsy as soon as possible."

The words had felt like a cold ocean wave, driving her under and dragging her against the sand. Breath came in gulps. Her heart raced. Before the appointment, Martha had been restless: middle-aged discontent with life. But the possibility of being pulled from it cut like a hot knife through life's obscuring veil of ordinariness. With its cloak fallen away, life stood, brilliant, before her. The sacredness of her family, the beauty of the world was painful to behold. Like Emily returned from her grave in *Our Town,* Martha wondered how she could have missed it before. What if she had cancer? How could she bear to let go of such splendor?

Her husband drove her to the hospital. Martha watched him. He had tried to reassure her: "I love you, always. That won't change if the worst happens and you lose a breast."

Martha tried to imagine looking in the mirror and seeing only

145

one breast. She pushed the image from her mind.

"Maybe he would still love me," she thought. "Would I?"

For the rest of the drive, she concentrated on praying for the doctors, nurses, and anesthesiologists who would be working with her. Praying for them as God's agents of healing had gotten her through the days of waiting. She wasn't comfortable praying too much for herself. God knew the problem. She didn't want to be like a whining child. Besides, people were suffering all over the world. More immediate dangers. When she did pray for herself, it was for grace to deal with whatever would come.

The days after the biopsy dragged by. By Monday she was waiting for the phone to ring.

"I have no reason to think the worst. No history of breast cancer in the family. No high-risk factors."

Then she thought about others she knew. Others who had no reason to think the worst, but who had fought and lost battles with cancer and heart disease. Vulnerable.

Martha watched her family. "How would they do without me?" she pondered. She knew they somehow would. They would struggle. They would hurt. But life would go on.

She hated those thoughts. They came suddenly, like a cloud burst, and flooded over her. At the craziest times: picking up a child from school; cooking dinner; her husband's kiss. Her eyes would fill with tears. She felt cold. Thoughts like that immobilized her. She had to force herself to keep pushing the cart or stirring the soup.

On Tuesday, she couldn't wait any longer. She called the doctor's office.

"You were on our list to call today," the nurse said. "The lump was benign."

The rest of the instructions were a distant buzz.

"Benign. No problem. A gift of life." Martha smiled. Her hands felt warm again.

~

How tenuous is our hold on life. How much we take for granted. In a moment, the fabric of our lives can unravel. Lord, still the racing of my heart. Calm my fears. Slow my racing mind that projects countless worries into our future. Help me hold on to you, the one thing I know for sure. Grace me with clarity of vision, to drink in the wonder of the life you have given me.

THE FLOWER

If we hope for what we do not yet have,
we wait for it patiently.
Romans 8:25

Eager first-graders gathered around their desks, examining the white carnations I had supplied for an experiment. One small and unkempt boy was particularly gentle as he held his.

"Is this a rose?" he asked. "It has lots of petals."

"Roses do have lots of petals, but this isn't a rose. It is a carnation."

He studied it, running his thin fingers over the petals.

"What's gonna happen, Mrs. Holt? Are they gonna grow?" a girl asked.

"I bet I know," said another. "They're gonna change color, aren't they, Mrs. Holt?"

"That's what we are going to find out. Does anyone else have a prediction?"

One child thought the carnations might sprout more flowers. Another thought they would grow roots. We discussed possibilities for a while, then proceeded with the steps of the experiment: pour water into graduated cylinders, add food coloring, cut the flower stem to an appropriate length and finally, place the carnations in the cylinders.

One by one all the students put their containers on a table except for the small boy who had held his flower with such care. He was sitting at his desk with the cylinder in front of him. His eyes never left the flower.

"What are you seeing, Matt?" I asked, squatting down beside him. My gaze followed his and fixed on the carnation.

He looked at me and smiled.

"Nothing, yet," he explained in a hushed voice. "But I will!"

~

Oh, for such expectant waiting! Lord, fill my heart with such faith and hope.

❧

PART SEVEN

ON THE ROAD

My husband has a small car for commuting to his office, thirty miles away. I have a minivan for carrying children, friends, and "stuff" from location to location. Living in a small city, I assumed his car would accumulate miles more quickly than mine. How far can it be to the high school and back, or to the grocery store? Certainly not sixty miles a day.

Surprise! My car is the one with the most miles. Little trips add up. I make lots of them. When we were first married, my husband accused me of shopping ingredient by ingredient. I said it was my European style of buying fresh produce and bread for the day, not the week. We laughed then. Marysville was a small town. Living right over the railroad tracks from a mom-and-pop grocery, a trip to the store for a forgotten green pepper or carton of milk meant a short, enjoyable walk.

Not anymore. Besides school and shopping there are runs to play practice and the library; to friends and family; to lessons and meets. The odometer clicks away and the gas station manager smiles as he rings up sale after sale. Our mobile lifestyle is making someone rich. How many hours a week do I spend behind the wheel of a car? Though I've never counted, I know: too many.

Yet time in the car often has its own gifts if we become aware of them. It can provide precious moments alone with my husband or children. The conversations that we have keep us in touch with each other. A piece on the radio or a sight out the window may seed thoughts to ponder throughout the day. For a mother who spends so much of her time behind the wheel, it's good to remember that God is with us there, too.

MAKING THE TIME
TO TALK

One must learn a different... sense of time, one that
depends more on small amounts than on big ones.[1]
Sr. Mary Paul

L ong car trips have often provided Rick and me with time to talk. The scenario has changed over the years, but many good conversations took place while we were traveling down highways.

Life gets busy, no matter the age or stage of your children. Over the years, long trips have helped us smooth the rough edges in our relationship. Inches away from each other for hours on end, we eventually had to allow safely submerged thoughts and feelings to surface.

When our children were young, packing the car was a major part of the trips: diaper bag, diapers, and lotions; portable crib, stroller, and food grinder; snacks, travel books, and favorite toys. No time to talk! That came later.

No matter how fussy the children were when we started out, they were good travelers, often asleep after twenty miles or so. Then came "our" time. Oblivious to scenery, we talked about all the things we hadn't had time to share. Unhurried time together was a gift.

Sometimes tears came as we touched on hurts and misunderstandings. Sometimes we discussed ideas or dreams. Whatever the conversation, we were closer to each other when we arrived at our destination than we were before the trip began. Even if we had not resolved a problem, at least we knew better how the other felt.

Now our children are older. They don't sleep away the miles. Conversations are often a family activity. Still, when Rick and I have the chance to travel in the car alone, we plan on time to talk and catch up with each other.

~

Once, when an unexpected day to spend together came along, we considered driving through Amish country to look for a table. I didn't want to spend the time traveling.

"I don't mind the drive," Rick said. "Besides, we could talk."

Rather than turning on the car radio or putting a tape in the player, we talk and listen. God provides snatches of time. We learn to grab it.

LIVING IN THE WORLD

In the world you will have trouble, but take courage,
I have conquered the world.
John 16:33

While in sixth grade, our daughter, Emily, strained under the weight of her increasing awareness of the world's dark side. A voracious reader, *Bullfinch's Mythology* and Shakespeare were already part of her "books read" list. However, she balked at novels chosen by her teacher. They dealt with child abuse, abandonment, and Nazi death camps. Coupled with grim headlines and suffering around the world, they were too heavy a burden for her sensitive nature and youthful expectation of fairness. "I know this stuff happens," she would say, "but I don't want to read about it!"

One morning as I was taking her to school, she began this conversation.

"I was thinking. I'd like to go off by myself. Like Sam in *My Side of the Mountain*. I'd like to find a place far away from cities and people. Someplace where I could live close to nature."

We stopped at a traffic light and then continued through downtown. "The world can be an ugly place sometimes, can't it?" I asked.

"Yes! Isn't there someplace we can go and grow up and live together without all the problems? Isn't there someplace where there are people like us? Where bad things don't happen? You know, like murders and child abuse. Where people don't talk about sex all the time and do things that ruin the earth and hurt people..." Her voice trailed off and she stared out the window.

"You know, Em, sometimes I wish that same thing, but I don't think such a place exists. When I feel like that, I try to remember that Jesus calls us to help heal the world. He counts on us to be partners with him. It isn't easy."

She sighed and looked at St. Mary's Church as we drove by.

"I guess," she said. She didn't sound convinced. "It's like being *in* the world and not *of* it, right?"

"Right. That's why faith is so important. I know I couldn't do it without Jesus' help. With it, I can. So can you. Battling evil is never easy, but it's important. Jesus wants you to use your gifts, too." Emily smiled a little. We arrived at school. Leaning over, I kissed her cheek. She got out of the car and began walking to the front door. She turned and waved, flashing her brilliant smile. I smiled back and watched her disappear into the building.

~

The world can be overwhelming for adults. Young people are forced to grapple with it at an early age. Lord, my daughter tries to deal with evil in the world. Sometimes she is frightened. Sometimes angry. Sometimes she'd like to run away from it all. Lord, strengthen her faith. Be with her as she chooses to be in the world and not of it. Give her your love to overcome the evil she encounters in her world.

THE LOVE THAT
BINDS US

*O Lord, support us all the daylong, until the shadows
lengthen and the evening comes, and the busy world is
hushed, and the frenzy of life is over, and our work is
done. Then in thy mercy grant us a safe lodging,
and a holy rest, and peace at the last.[2]*
Book of Common Prayer

"I don't understand why you take your children to school and
pick them up when they could ride the bus. It stops right in
front of your house."

That comment has been made to me a number of times.
Sometimes a friend is trying to help lighten my busy schedule.
After looking at our gas bill, my husband has made similar
remarks. I used to try explaining. Now I just smile, nod and continue to drive my children to school. Unless they ride with us,
others will not understand: the children and I share wonderful
conversations on those runs.

Some mornings we chuckle all the way to school. Once an
oldies radio station was playing a song from the late sixties. As I
reminisced about peace rallies and coffee houses, my teens listened with skepticism and amusement. "You really did that,
Mom?" I guess they couldn't picture me in bell bottoms and
beads, playing a guitar. We joked about fashion then and now.

The question "Did you see last night's Calvin and Hobbes?"
can lead us to recite our favorites and laugh all over again.

On other mornings the conversations are more serious. We

discuss current events or challenges of growing up in the nineties; peer pressures, pending tests, or the jarring reality of a classmate getting pregnant. Sometimes we are silent. Though each with our own thoughts, we still are together; a quiet support for the beginning day. We have marveled at icicles hanging from sandstone outcroppings or dogwoods that make spring hillsides look dappled with snow.

Rides home are equally rich. They are times when the day's news, good or bad, is shared. The familiar van offers a friendly embrace after a day in the world. Ideas that have been fermenting, plans for the afternoon, problems to deal with, all come spilling out in the safe environs.

Why would I want to give up such times? If someone asks why I run my children to school, I assume they have not had the pleasure.

~

Thank you, Lord, for these times between waking up and becoming immersed in our worlds of school, home, and work. They are interludes between schedules when we rest in the relationships and love that bind us together. They are times to be family in a busy world.

Help me find such times for you and me.

AND A LITTLE CHILD
SHALL LEAD THEM

*Christ hungers now, my brethren; it is he who deigns to
hunger and thirst in the persons of the poor.*[3]
Caesarius of Arles

The cold autumn air bit through our jackets as we climbed
into the family van. Shivering until the car warmed up, we
enjoyed the half hour drive into Columbus; the science museum
was holding an evening open house for members, showcasing the
newest exhibit. Time passed quickly. We didn't expect the turn of
events that awaited us.

As we exited the freeway and pulled up to the traffic light, a
couple sitting on the sidewalk caught our attention. Wrapped in a
blanket, they held a hand-lettered sign: "Will work for food."

We live in a small town where such sights are not common.
Looking away, embarrassed by the encounter, I remembered the
advice of a nun I had once interviewed. She worked with homeless people in Washington, D.C. She told me they feel invisible.
People who see them don't know what to do. They are uncomfortable, so they look away. "Smile at them," she said. My
thoughts were interrupted by our nine-year-old.

"What are we going to do?" she asked. I turned and looked at
her face. Tears were watering her eyes. "I know what I am going
to do when I'm grown-up. I'm going to have a big house and let
all the homeless people live there until they have someplace to
go."

My husband, Rick, turned toward the museum.

"What should we do now?" Kathryn insisted.

"Maybe we could give them some money," one of the children suggested.

Rick looked at me and I nodded. He turned the van around in a parking lot and headed back to the freeway bridge. He stopped the car along a sidestreet.

"Josh and I will go talk to them," he said. "We'll see what we can do."

They got out of the car and disappeared around the corner.

"I remember seeing a man sleeping over a grate in Washington last year. Do you remember, Mom?" Kathryn asked.

I did. While we waited for them to return, we talked about homelessness, and what we could do to help. More questions than answers. After fifteen minutes, Rick and Josh came back. They had talked to the couple and given them some money. We drove off to the museum and waved to the man and woman as we passed by.

~

How easily we become accustomed to suffering around us, or view such requests for help with skepticism. If Kathryn had not been upset, we would have driven by the couple on the bridge. We might have felt guilty, embarrassed, or cynical, but we would have continued on our way.

Our youngest remembered the words she had heard about "doing something for the least of my people." She had been taught that helping others was a way of helping Jesus. If we had driven on without responding to the people on the bridge, all the words we had spoken, or would ever speak, about serving the Lord in his people would sound hollow to her ears.

Thank you, Lord, for our young daughter's faith. Where I saw two people asking for money, she saw you in need and responded with her heart.

"WE'RE A TEAM"

*But while he was still a long way off, his father saw him
and was filled with compassion for him; he ran to his son,
threw his arms around him and kissed him.*
Luke 15:20

Pointing the car down the dark road, she gripped the steering wheel and looked over at her teenage son. He sat close to the door, staring out the window. It had not been an easy night. First had been the phone call:

"Hello. This is Officer Woodsley. Is this Mrs. Shane?"

"Yes."

"Are you Jerry Shane's mother?"

"Yes, I am."

"Is he at home?"

She had looked at her son sitting on the couch. He watched her, his face white, his hands clenched.

"Yes he is. May I ask what this is about?"

"We'd like you to come down to the station with him. There's been an incident on Jackson St. We have reason to believe your son was involved. We'd like to ask him some questions in your presence."

Next came the long conversation. She had decided to get the story firsthand before they left the house. "I want the truth," she had said. "Every fact. Every detail. I don't want any surprises when we're down there. We're a team. I'll support you all I can. But if we get there and I find out you haven't told me everything, then you're on your own."

He told her everything. She could see the fear in his face. He

161

knew her anger. But, after twenty minutes, the anger had begun to drain away. He was her son. He had made a mistake. They would go together. He would face the consequences, but nothing he didn't deserve.

As she drove to the station she looked at him. Her heart was racing. She was sure his was, too. Wondering what would happen. Questions. Doubts. What had gone wrong?

Still, in the midst of it all, she knew something had gone right. There was no wall between them. No belligerence. No deceit. She was thankful for the quiet ride. It gave them time to collect their thoughts. She breathed a silent prayer of thanks for the relationship they had built over the years that made honesty possible. She asked for strength, patience, and wisdom to handle what would come. She looked again at her son. He turned his face toward her. She saw the sorrow and apprehension that had replaced his youthful bravado. Their eyes met. She tried a smile.

"I'm sorry, Mom."

"I know," she said. "We'll get through. We're a team."

~

I wonder at my friend's handling of a difficult situation. Would I be as strong? As understanding? Would I be as supportive, or would I get lost in my own hurt and anger? Wanting to distance myself from the sinner as well as the sin?

Lord, grant me a generous spirit that loves with no thought for itself. That desires only to be a channel of your redeeming love.

NATURE

On a day early one May, when I was still a college student, I took a camera and headed into the Hocking Hills area south of my home. In search of something to share with my mother for Mother's Day, I scouted the woods and roadside, finding trillium, bluettes, and yellow coneflowers. I spent hours looking, photographing, and resting against the old oak and maple trees.

Taking photographs of ordinary things has long been a kind of prayer for me. I didn't do it often. Unlike professional photographers, who shoot rolls at a time, I would get lost in contemplating the flower or root, or peeling paint on a fire hydrant, and forget to take pictures.

The genuineness of ordinary things speaks to me of purity of heart. The most common rock and flower, the oldest tree or tangle of vines, the gothic church or weathered barn. Because they are just as they were made to be, they need no adornment or arranging by human hands. They sing out a great "Amen." A "Yes" to the Creator. So, they give glory to their Maker.

In *New Seeds of Contemplation,* Thomas Merton says, "A tree gives glory to God by being a tree. For in being what God means it to be it is obeying Him."[1] From ancient times until today, the beauty, power, and mystery of nature have inspired humanity to great works: artists to express their experience, scientists to search for understanding, philosophers to ponder, contemplatives to pray.

It is that faithfulness of the natural world to the Creator that fills those who see with reverence and awe. By its pure reflection of God's artistry and creative power, it moves us to prayer and reveals some facet of the Maker to his people. When we open our eyes, ears, and hearts to the wordless chant of praise that arises every day from every created thing, we can join in their prayer. Recognizing their holiness, our own hearts are stirred with the desire to grow in willingness to be, like them, exactly as God has made us to be. Then our "Amen" will rise with theirs, not from our lips alone, but from our being.

DESERT TIMES

I shall and shall not be with you. I shall clothe you in My Grace, but you will think yourself deprived of it, because while dwelling within you I shall be able to go unrecognized. I am concealing myself from you so that you may discover by yourself what you are without Me.[2]
Margaret of Cortona

I sat by a small creek winding its way along the base of a hill. The clear water gurgled as it fell over rocks in its way. Closing my eyes, I tried to still my spirit and pray. But instead of turning to quiet meditation, my mind filled with myriad thoughts and concerns: children, school, book deadlines, a summer course I was teaching, a misunderstanding with my husband. They tumbled into consciousness, one on top of the other.

I tried slow, rhythmic breathing. The Jesus Prayer. All the techniques I could remember, but nothing worked. My spirit was as turbulent as the stream.

Did Jesus feel like this when he was in the desert? He went there to pray and to fast. Perhaps some of his time was spent sitting on a rock, trying to focus, trying to hear his father, but hearing nothing.

Forcing my eyes to look at the creek, I listened to it and watched the sun glint off the surface. As the water rushed by, the thoughts and worries cleared slowly from my mind.

Still at last. I sat. No great prayer rose in my heart. No religious experience. No sense of God speaking eloquently through creation, or even whispering in the wind. Nothing. Just a glazed feeling in my mind, the feeling I get sometimes when I can't focus my eyes. They stare ahead, not locking in on anything.

My spirit was not soaring to God and God's Spirit did not seem to be getting through to me. I had gone to the creek hoping to break out of daily routines which seemed empty. I had hoped to connect with God, His energy and His Love.

Instead I sat with nothing but the feeling of being alone.

~

Lord, help me accept the desert times. The empty times. Only trusting that God is working deep within me makes them bearable. Light cannot illuminate that which is already radiant. God will come into my desert soul and make it bloom. I must wait and let him work.

MONET'S SUNRISE

The heavens are telling the glory of God,
And the firmament proclaims his handiwork.
Psalm 19:1

"Mom! Mom!"

I turned over in my bed. Through sleepy eyes I saw a bleary image of my daughter, Kathryn, standing beside me.

"Mom," she whispered again, "would you watch the sunrise with me, like Monet did?"

My eyes began to focus. I could see the expectant look on her face. She had become keenly interested in Monet, his paintings, and all things French. That particular morning, she had decided to get up early and observe a sunrise from our front porch. She had invited me to share the experience. How could a mother refuse such an invitation? How often are we grown-ups included in such serendipitous moments? I am not an early riser. Sunsets are more compatible with my schedule. Getting out of bed, I pulled on jeans and a T-shirt. We walked through the living room. I grabbed an afghan for each of us, and together we stepped onto the front porch.

We snuggled close in our blankets and leaned our backs against the house. In silence, we watched. Night's cold seeped from the concrete porch, chilling us through the afghans. Suddenly, the sky was painted with rose, pink, purple, and bright blue. In minutes, the colors moved across the sky. Still silent, we witnessed the common miracle.

"This happens every morning," I thought to myself, "and I sleep through it!"

"How does he do it?" Kathryn asked. "How does Monet get the paint to look like this?"

We both sat awash in the morning's glory. When the sun was up and the sky was tame again we went inside for a cup of tea.

~

How many sunrises have I slept through? How may sunsets have I missed? A friend once told me he'd never missed a sunrise in his life. I could see why. Still, I know I will continue to sleep as late as I can before beginning a new day.

I am often oblivious to the beauty and wonder of God's hand in creation. I don't stop to marvel at beaded edges of grass on a dewy morning, the delicate lace of a spider's web, or the unfolding of springtime leaves.

Lord, give me eyes to see the reflection of your glory in the natural world around me.

AN OCTOBER MORNING

And thou shalt be secure, because there is hope.
Job 11:10 KJV

Sometimes the beauty of October in central Ohio is too much for me. It pours in through my eyes and overflows my soul. Like the morning my daughter and I drove thirty miles to Columbus for an early appointment.

While driving up the road, we marveled at the red sunrise, the rainbow on our left, the blue sky on our right. The grassy strip dividing the highway was thick and green. Like a National Geographic photograph of Ireland, the grass looked as if it had a light of its own, illuminating its color from the inside out.

Slender strands of copper rose like reeds along the edges of the green. They were plants, grown tall and gone to seed. On our left were stretches of long, light-brown grasses that softened the space where field and roadside met. Yellow goldenrod and purple asters mixed together along fence rows.

"I don't often come up here so early in the morning," my daughter said. "We're lucky we came today. Isn't it beautiful?"

It was. It reminded me that in the midst of a world full of problems, good things, beautiful things, hopeful things are happening. The sun comes up, the earth keeps turning, and every day is a chance to do better at something. Children are learning to read and to make new friends and to pump the swings all by themselves.

Somewhere, couples have fought and are learning to forgive, someone is playing Mozart, and an artist is dipping a brush into paint. A harvest is good, a stream is full of fish, and the air is full of birds that know which way is south. Someone has recovered from an illness, and another's spirits have risen from the darkest of places.

Somewhere, mothers are picking up babies; fathers have paused to listen to their sons. A cool drink of water has eased a fever. A visit has cheered a lonely soul.

"Mom, is it always this pretty; I mean early in the morning?" my daughter said.

I had to admit I didn't know. If I were looking with an October heart, my answer would be "yes."

~

How easy it is to become disheartened in a world scourged with evil and its issue. Doubt slips into the heart even when we want to believe that good is in the world, and in ourselves.

October mornings are not always as magnificent as the one I shared with my daughter. Rainbows don't always hang from the clouds and rain isn't always falling somewhere to the west. Sometimes it is pelting down, cold and hard, on us. Still, each sunrise brings a new day. God is still with us. Even when we don't notice, nature's beauty and tenacity tells me not to give up, because God hasn't.

FOCUSING ON
THE PRESENT

Yesterday is ashes; tomorrow wood.
Only today does the fire burn brightly.[3]
Old Eskimo Saying

The approaching deadline meant the column on my desk needed to be finished, but no words came. No ideas. Taking off my glasses, I looked up from the paper and stared out the window. Sentences were mentally composed and discarded as I searched for the thought that would set words flowing again.

I don't know how long I sat there, looking at blowing leaves and birds flitting from tree to tree by the creek bed. Suddenly, I became aware of the vase of flowers on my desk. I had been staring past them all the while as I looked out the window. A blur of form and color, they came into sharp focus, as if my mind were a camera shifting its depth of field. The creek and trees became a mottled green backdrop to burgundy snapdragons' velvety blooms.

How could I have looked past something so elegant without noticing? For the next few minutes, I explored their captivating shapes and shadow; their line and color. Then, as if whispered to me by the flowers, words came again.

~

How often do I stare past things of great beauty because my attention is riveted somewhere else? Often I lose the beauty of

171

people and things and moments close at hand because my focus is in the future. It might be concern about tomorrow's work or the evening's dinner or a college choice looming ahead. I am lost in thought, focused far away. What is closest is a blur.

Help me, Lord, to see what you have placed before me. Your beauty and intricacies are before me always in the people and world you have made.

Help me take time to focus on the present. I will not find you when I am lost in the search for what is to come.

CHANGE ON THE CREEK

One cannot step twice into the same river.
Herclitus

The morning was clear and cold. The sun, climbing in the blue sky, had not yet risen over the tallest ridge. Still, it glistened on the ice crystals that had grown during the frigid night on every branch, weed, and bent blade of grass.

I decided to take a walk up the small valley beside the cabin. The sound of rushing water surprised me.

Crossing over to the creek that ran along the foot of the hill, I noticed how much wider it had become since my last visit. Swollen from earlier days of melting snow and rain, it rushed over the large sandstone rocks and fell a foot or two before continuing its journey.

The extreme cold of the night before had worked with an artist's hand, edging the creek with frozen borders of transparent fleurs-de-lis.

Shallow ice "dishes" clung to the clumps of grass and moss on which they were formed and resisted the push of the water. They were as clear as any fine crystal. Beginning at the smooth center, the cluster of rounded lobes fanned out like molten glass pulled gently by a master glassblower.

A sound like a footstep startled me. I looked to see if someone was coming. No. The sound was the cracking of the sheet ice that covered part of the creek upstream. Dark lines appeared, running the length of the ice. Warming morning was changing all.

As I stood watching, the cold seeped through my shoes. I

watched as the sheet ice cracked and buckled and began to break away. I watched as water finally eroded the icy pedestals that held the crystal dishes in place. One by one, they fell with the water, over the little falls, shattering into the creek below. I watched as the sun melted the diamonds off the trees, and felt a tinge of regret. The creek would never look exactly that way again.

~

The creek did not mourn its passing glory. It rushed ahead. The water that had been frozen for a while, in a pose surpassing human artistry, flowed anew. It may find its way back into ice again, but not before it has become drink for leafing trees or home for tadpoles or rain over the ocean.

Nature is not afraid of change.

Lord, help me be so gracious and trusting with the changes in my life. The same master Artist who sculpted the morning is at work in me. Creation knows the cycle. Dying and rising, dying and rising. Until we all stand true and clear as the morning's ice and become witness to the final glory that is God.

THE HUMMINGBIRD

Faith is the substance of things hoped for,
the evidence of things not seen.
Hebrews 11:1 KJV

I bought a hummingbird feeder for the study window. Nothing fancy. Held onto the glass with a suction cup, it sticks out like a red, plastic hockey puck.

I filled it with sugar water and waited. I emptied it every few days and refilled it with fresh syrup and waited some more. Nothing. To make the area more attractive to hummers, I planted bee balm under the window. Faithfully, I tended garden and feeder.

One day as I sat writing, a dark form flitted across the edge of my vision. Slowly, not wanting to frighten a possible visitor, I raised my head and turned to look. There was my long-awaited guest, its body more delicate than I had remembered. Its long, slender beak dipped in and out of the red feeder. I watched for a few seconds. Then it was gone.

Every few days for the rest of the season, I changed the sugar water. I never saw the hummingbird again. I didn't need to. I knew it was there, somewhere.

~

I don't need to see something or be aware of its presence for it to be real. I don't have to be aware of God visiting my soul for him to come. I only need to keep my soul ready for his visit.

175

THE FLOWER
GARDEN

❧

*All we know for sure is that God is fashioning a mas-
terpiece of unimaginable beauty way beneath what
the human eye can see or the human mind can com-
prehend. Only in time as the plan begins to take
shape will hints of what is taking place beneath the
surface begin to emerge.*[4]

Fr. Joseph F. Girzone

Outside our kitchen door is a small garden space. Early in the
spring, I loosened the soil and planted flowers. The snapdragons, asters, and pinks were seedlings. The rest were started
from seed: bachelor buttons, a few marigolds, dependable zinnias. They fill in the empty spaces around the perennial lavender,
columbine, and flax. I like flowers that grow tall, look a bit
unkempt, and make lovely bouquets in the summer. So, I
planned and planted.

One corner bloomed first. A small cluster of blue flax and
some yellow coreopsis were the perfect backdrop for bright red
carnations. At the opposite end of the garden, an old lavender
plant began shooting up fragrant foliage with the promise of
bloom in its tightly closed buds.

After its first burst of color, the garden limped through summer. The asters, labeled "tall, perfect for cutting," turned out to
be dwarf plants. Few flowered. The snapdragons did not bush
out as they usually do, and only a few bachelor buttons germinat-
ed. A wild columbine, given by a friend, bloomed and threatened

176

to take over and the zinnias, my least favorite, yielded the most blooms.

The garden looked spotty at best. I looked in vain for the flowers I had planted. Disappointed, I'd pick a bouquet of zinnias with a token snapdragon or two and place them around the house.

One afternoon, while staring at the patch from the steps outside the kitchen, I realized that if I would forget the garden I carried around in my head, the one I had wasn't so bad.

The zinnias added lots of color. The lavender had spread and was full of blooms. Even if few, the red and yellow snapdragons were tall. If trimmed, the coreopsis would bloom all summer. I just had to learn to love the garden that grew, not the one I planted!

～

Life does not always unfold as we plan or imagine. Lord, help me accept the imperfections, changes, and unexpected in my own life. Teach me to embrace what I am given, and not waste time grieving for what might have been.

FLOOD RELIEF

❧

We are hard pressed on every side, but not crushed;
perplexed, but not in despair; persecuted, but not
abandoned; struck down, but not destroyed.
2 Corinthians 4:8-9

"Will peanut butter be OK?" asked my daughter.

"Yes, and put in those cans of soup and tunafish, too." We were gathering non-perishable foods from our pantry to take to the drop box in our grocery store parking lot.

"How will they heat the soup, Mom? They don't have any electricity."

"They will soon," I answered.

Once again floods had hit. Locations change, but rains and storms come every year: hurricanes on the coastlines, tornados and thunderstorms inland.

A few years ago we had a clogged drainage pipe and water backed up in the basement. It was only an inch or two and it receded quickly. The cleanup was time-consuming, but nothing of value was lost. Still, everything smelled damp and musty for a while. As we packed up food for flood victims I tried to imagine seeing two or three feet of water in my home and fording streets that looked like rivers.

How do people come back and face the horrible mess a flood makes in a home: the mud halfway up walls, the furniture and appliances ruined? So much had been lost. So much was covered in silt, slime, and sewage.

A friend lived close to this latest flood. I called every couple of days to see how she was doing. People who had been flooded out a number of times, only to return and rebuild, knowing the next flood was only time away, puzzled me. Why would they want to stay?

Kathryn's call broke into my reverie.

"I think that's it, Mom. Let's go."

We took the bags out to the car and drove to the grocery store. What looked like a lot of food at home seemed small as we placed it into the large collection box. I thought I should go into the store and buy mops, soap, and buckets to send as well. When the water receded, they would need more than food to keep going.

~

Nature is harsh in its excesses. I don't know if I would have the courage and determination to face rebuilding after living through such a disaster. Bless those who do suffer in natural disasters. I am eager to send what relief I can: food, money, prayers. It's a small exchange for the faith and courage exported by those who refuse to give up despite overwhelming hardship. Their example helps me keep my own small crises in perspective.

PART NINE

❧

MODERN
SACRAMENTALS

In fifth grade, after successfully selling five books of Holy Childhood stamps, I came home proudly carrying my prize: a large black and gold plastic crucifix. My father pounded a nail in the wall over my bed where I solemnly hung the crucifix and looked around the bedroom. My oldest sister had a wooden cross that slid open and held candles and oils for an anointing. That was impressive. Guardian angel plaques, a picture of the Sacred Heart, and a holy water font hung on the walls. We had rosaries draped on our bedposts and a little statue of Mary on the dresser. At last I had a fine cross to add to the collection of sacramentals.

Our Catholic home was full of sacramentals. (Besides the black and gold crucifix, my favorite was the glow-in-the-dark statues of the Infant of Prague.) We had stacks of holy cards garnered for good behavior or performance from the nuns at school. The liturgical year in our home began with the Advent wreath and continued with a crèche, palms, Easter Eggs, and May Altars.

Today my home is appointed with many of the same things. Our statues look friendlier than the ones I remember. Jesus has children in his lap and Mary holds her child playfully in the air. Story Bibles, prayer books, and lives of the saints rest on end tables and in bookshelves. We even have a couple of glow-in-the-dark rosaries.

However, traditional sacramentals are not the only ones to grace our home. Others, unrecognized by friends and visitors, are part of my daily life. Not found in religious stores, they speak eloquently of the Sacred Presence in our lives. Coffee mugs, a photograph, and a favorite rock have the power to turn my mind and heart to God. They bring me to prayer.

Teilhard de Chardin said, "Nothing is profane to those who know how to see it." For those who have eyes to see, everything can witness to the glory of God. In my daily life, there are objects that have become especially blessed sacramentals. Some have been gifts, while others are treasures offered by the earth.

Every home is blessed with these "modern sacramentals." They may not be recognized as channels of grace, but they are. Pouring tea from the teapot that graced a great aunt's table can be a moment of connection not only with family, but with God's grace that has flowed through it for generations. A rock brought home from England brings to mind not only memories of a trip, but of the expanse and variety of God's creation.

God desires to be with us all ways and everywhere. It is no surprise that even the most ordinary objects constantly call us to remember that, and to respond.

A CONSTANT COMPANION

The light of God surrounds me,
The love of God enfolds me,
The power of God protects me,
The Presence of God watches over me,
Wherever I am, God is.
Prayer Card

When my children were young we struggled with an over-population of stuffed animals. They filled bags in the storage space under the eaves. They congregated at the bottoms of beds and lined up along the walls. They rode in cars, were dragged into tree houses, and stared at me with their unblinking eyes from behind the couch. They were the stuffed animals that arrived wrapped with ribbons and pretty paper. They came from amusement parks, toy stores, and garage sales. A few were given to St. Vincent De Paul's. Most stayed. In moments of exasperation, I voiced my desire to get rid of them all. My children stared at me, horror-struck, and offered immediate objections:

"Brown Bear's from Grandpa!"

"Dad gave me this when I was born, remember? He brought Rabbit to the hospital. You told me."

"But he is so soft!"

A few were relegated to storage for awhile and eventually reappeared as they were missed and returned to the beds.

I had been puzzled by such fierce attachment until one particular incident helped me understand. It occurred when our youngest was four years old.

Dragging her stuffed animal, Carbell, Kathryn had come with me to her sister's class on a field trip. Somehow during the day and subsequent visit to an aunt's house, we lost Carbell. We searched everywhere. I called parents who had driven on the field trip. Teachers looked in coat rooms and lost and found boxes. No Carbell.

For a year Kathryn grieved. She lit candles at church and prayed for Carbell's return. At children's liturgy her petition was for her beloved stuffed animal to come home.

"Carbell is the only thing I ever won at a fair all by myself," Kathryn confided in me one day. Her eyes filled with tears. "And I love her."

Sitting Kathryn on my lap, I held her while tears flowed.

"When I get to heaven," she said, "the first thing I'm going to ask God is 'where is Carbell?'"

I didn't doubt it.

~

Stuffed animals are much more to children than they appear to be. They have shared scary nights and tea parties, laughter and tears. They have heard and kept countless secrets and complaints about the grownups and their world. The stuffed animals were always there. To listen and to comfort.

In their humble way they are a reflection of the loving, affirming presence of our God. A friend who loves to listen, the one who is our constant companion.

Lord, help me respect my children's sacramentals. They are different than my own. Whatever they are, they offer some sense of constancy and reassurance in a world that is sometimes challenging and baffling to the younger ones. Someday, they will understand that You are the source of all love. You are the One we can turn to for comfort and hope.

ON MY WINDOWSILL

❧

A bruised reed he shall not break, and a
smoldering wick he shall not quench.
Isaiah 42:3

Standing at the sink for what must have been the tenth time that day, I fantasized about having a more prestigious job, one that would not include the endless task of keeping a family kitchen clean. My gaze drifted to the windowsill in front of me. A motley collection crowded its narrow ledge. Dusty. "Just get rid of all the little stuff," I thought to myself. "It makes keeping this place neat that much harder."

I reached for the liquid soap. The bottle tipped and knocked a small disk into the dish water. Quickly, I fished it out and ran it under warm water. Before replacing it, I examined it. One of a pair, it was an irregular, flat black oval. Carefully pressed onto it were silhouettes of the moon and a star. Its partner was still on the shelf. Same shape. Light blue. Decorated with a sun.

I remembered my daughter giving them to me. They were her symbols of night and day. She knew I liked to watch the sky; she was offering it to me in her own way.

I replaced it on the windowsill next to a small piece of green chalk that had been turned on a makeshift lathe until it resembled a gumball machine. Smiling, I remembered how our son made his first lathe years ago. He fashioned pencils into undulating spindles. His favorites, though, were the chalk sculptures. How many times had I scooped that up out of the dish water, afraid it would dissolve!

While I worked, I looked over the collection on the sill. Suddenly, the dishes were finished. I wrung out the cloth and

185

hung it over the edge of the sink to dry. The kitchen was as clean as it would get that day. The windowsill would stay as it was.

~

My windowsill is lined with gifts of self. It is not clay symbols of night and day or a chalk gumball machine that line my windowsill. It is the love of a daughter, a son, a husband, a friend. All becoming vulnerable by sharing something of themselves with me. They know their gifts are small and imperfect yet they risk giving them anyway. They want to connect, to give and be received; to love and be loved.

Lord, like a child, I offer you my self, my work, done with all my heart. Although it is flawed and small, you receive it with joy. That you hold me, imperfect as I am, gives me courage to continue to grow in your love and grace. Help me hold the gifts of self my loved ones entrust to me.

UNEXPECTED SHARING

*It is only with the heart that one can see rightly;
what is essential is invisible to the eye.[1]*
Antoine de Saint-Exupéry

My desk, journals, and office bulletin board are sprinkled
with notes and drawings from my children. A few days ago
while cleaning the study, I found a painting that had slipped
through the crack between the desk and the window. The picture
was a watercolor with a large, yellow-brown head of a lion in the
center. The mane was glorious in wide, bold strokes. Carefully
hand-lettered in red were the words: "Remember, Aslan has to
come sometime."

I picked up the painting and hung it with magnets on the side
of the file cabinet. For years I had looked at it and remembered
C.S. Lewis' stories of the land of Narnia. In one, Aslan, the great
lion from beyond the sea, redeems the kingdom from the reign
of the White Witch. He willingly dies for a traitor in order to
break the witch's powers. He rises again, his own power rooted in
the deeper, ancient magic that gave rise to all worlds.

The admonition "Remember, Aslan has to come sometime"
encouraged me to hope and have faith that Jesus will not forsake
me. Even when I cannot see how or when, I know he will come
sometime.

Trying to remember what prompted such an insightful remark
from a child, I asked one night at dinner who had made me that
lovely painting of Aslan.

"I did." Kathryn spoke right away.

I told her how I had treasured it over the years, and shared
what its message meant to me.

"That's not what it means," Kathryn objected. "Don't you remember? We were reading it and everyone in the story was sad and hoping for Aslan to come back. Then for lots of nights, you forgot to read. I wanted to find out what happened, so I made the picture. I was telling you to keep reading because Aslan had to come sometime."

We all laughed.

"Well, it means something else to me now!" I said.

~

God shares himself in the most unexpected ways. Our children's notes and drawings often help me focus on some truth of faith that is lost through my fragmented, grown-up view.

ORDINARY THINGS

The earth is the Lord's, and everything in it,
the world, and all who live in it.
Psalm 24:1

I choose a coffee mug with care from our eclectic collection. Each one directs my thoughts in a different direction. Which one holds the morning's brew depends on my mood or situation.

One is white, wrapped with a meadow of flowers. The psalmist's words—"This is the day the Lord has made, let us rejoice and be glad"—circle the cup. On mornings that are particularly lacking in promise, the words form a prayer for one who wants to believe.

Another is covered with a heat-sensitive map of Pangaea. When hot water is added, the map changes to show the earth as it is today. I ponder creation's mystery and the unimaginable time it spans as I watch it change. Emblazoned with a quote from Emerson about the meaning of success, a small mug invites me to correct priorities that have become misaligned. We have whale mugs, cat mugs, and mugs that celebrate occasions. Mugs from monasteries, stores, and work. My morning cup of tea can make a statement for those who care to look.

~

After backpacking through Europe as a teenager, I brought back ordinary things I could use often: kitchen towels, a shirt, colored pencils, a book, a half-sized guitar. Every time I used them, I remembered the trip, my traveling companion, and the friends we made.

Thank you, Lord, for common things that turn my heart and mind to you. Thank you for the little things that bring me to prayer.

THE BOAT

ஒ

*In weather for example, this translated into what is only
half-jokingly known as the Butterfly Effect — the notion
that a butterfly stirring the air today in Peking can
transform storm systems next month in New York.²*
James Gleick

Our neighbor Paul was dying of cancer. Not sick enough to
stay in bed, he spent much time resting or sitting at the
kitchen table. We missed seeing him working in his garage where
it seemed like he was always building or fixing something for
someone. After the children boarded the morning school bus, I
went over and shared tea and conversation with him.

I don't remember what we began talking about on that particular morning, but somehow we ended up swapping stories of little gifts we had given or received over our lifetimes. A smile
spread across his face. He looked at me with eyes that had just
been back to his mother's kitchen as he remembered it, fifty years
ago.

"Once I carved my mother a little boat out of a stick of
cedar," he began. "I was always whittling. Can't remember if I
gave it to her for her birthday or Christmas. But she loved it."

He paused, remembering its shape and line. Looking at his
hands, I could imagine them young, holding a knife and fashioning a boat. Since I had known him, he'd made a beautiful set of
cherry cabinets and a small hutch for their kitchen. It had glass
doors and displayed his wife's good dishes. Paul was always making something.

"It was a nice little boat," he continued. "Mom kept it for

191

years. She showed it to people when they came to visit. She had it until one of the grandchildren took it to school for show-and-tell and lost it."

He shook his head.

"She hated that."

Sitting in silence, we sipped our tea. I looked at him. Once round and rosy, his face was thin. His skin was yellow. Liver cancer. When he looked up, he smiled. For a moment his eyes sparkled like they had before the cancer began taking its toll.

"It was just a little boat, but she kept it for all those years."

~

Small gifts, small acts of kindness send ripples out that touch hearts and change lives more than we can imagine. I have no idea what that small boat meant to Paul's mother. What thoughts it brought to her mind. What smiles to her face.

That his mother had treasured his boat, proudly displaying it for so many years and grieving at its loss, touched her son's heart deeply. She could not have known that such simple appreciation would bring comfort and joy to him fifty years later as he sat at a kitchen table, battling cancer and sharing tea with a neighbor.

Lord, thank you for small gifts and great love with which they are given and received.

THE PHOTOGRAPH

Every person is Christ for me.[3]
Mother Teresa

After sorting through accumulated mail and reorganizing the ceramic bowl and assortment of interesting rocks and shells, I sprayed the buffet's glass cover with cleaner. Two weeks of dust and smudges disappeared under my rag. Before replacing the plants, I bent over to look at the photograph someone had slipped under the glass.

My father sat at the picnic table in his backyard. A cake celebrating his seventy-fifth birthday was blazing away. Surrounded by children and grandchildren, Dad was smiling. White hair framed his tanned face. His hands, criss-crossed with thick veins, still looked strong. How much had he done with them? Working for his family, fixing cars, mending toys, and carrying children. I studied the faces of my brothers and sisters, their spouses and children. Twenty-nine of us! Mom must have taken the picture. We tease her about recording every family gathering. Looking at the picture, I was glad she does. The camera can't capture the relationships and life we all share. But its pictures make me stop and consider the intricacies of love and commitment that bind my family together.

~

Despite my good intentions, envelopes of photographs pile up in drawers and boxes at my house. Rolls of undeveloped film sit inside the secretary desk. When I look at the one under the buffet glass, I resolve once again to put the rest in an album.

193

Photographs give us a chance to see the web of relationships, celebrations, and accomplishments that connect our lives with so many others. They help us remember the beauty of creation in the backyard as well as in faraway places.

Contemplating photographs can be prayer. God's image emerges through those of the people and places I see.

GOD IN OUR SOULS

❧

*Then the soul is in God and God in the soul, just as
the fish is in the sea and the sea in the fish.*
Catherine of Siena

The smooth, shiny interior curled away into the mystery of
the old lightning whelk shell. Years of tumbling in ocean salt
and sand had smoothed its broken edges. Black lines, like fine
pen-and-ink strokes etched its chalky surface.

At first glance they suggested imagery, a picture needing only a
few more details to emerge. As it was, their randomness was
pleasing. Their intricacy reflected the world from which it came.

I found the shell one morning as I walked the beach. The hard
sand near the water was glazed by retreating waves. It reflected
sandpipers breakfasting on sand fleas and coquinas. Watery clouds
looked up at their rosy counterparts in the sky. Churning water
pounded the shore, chanting the ageless mantra of the sea. The
rhythm erased my sense of time as effortlessly as the water at my
ankles floated footprints away.

The jetty, a misty shadow in the distance, was suddenly
beneath my feet. I didn't remember walking so far. Time loses
meaning at the beach. All that remains is Presence. The Power
that moves the ocean. The Life that fills it. The Breath that sends
the salty air blowing across the dunes.

~

Presence. I wonder if heaven is like morning by the sea. A life
where time is transcended, like the other dimensions, and we are

195

196 ALL EARTH IS CRAMMED WITH HEAVEN

awash in the Presence of the One Who Is, like shells awash in the ocean.

Presence. That is the message of the lightning whelk. I took it off my kitchen windowsill, and sent it to a dying friend. It reminded us both: we are connected by the One who surrounds all.

NOTES

Introduction

1. Elizabeth Barrett Browning, "Auora Leigh," in *The Poetical Works of Elizabeth Barrett Browning*, edited by Harriet Waters Preston, (New York: Houghton Mifflin, 1974), 372.

Part 1: Family

1. Julian of Norwich, *Showings* (New York: Paulist, 1978), 130.
2. Abraham Heschel, *I Asked For Wonder* (New York: Crossroad, 1986), 57.
3. Teresa of Avila, in *Quotable Saints* (Ann Arbor, Mich.: Servant, 1992), 129-30.
4. Byzantine Rite of Betrothal, *Byzantine Missal*, Rev. Joseph Raya and Baron José de Vinck (Tournai, Belgium: Société Saint Jean L'Evangeliste Deselée and Cie, 1958), 727.
5. Madeleine L'Engle, *Two-Part Invention* (San Francisco: Harper & Row, 1989), 181.
6. Pierre Teilhard de Chardin, *The Phenomenon of Man* (New York: Harper-Collins, 1975).
7. Rabindranath Tagore, *Stray Birds* as quoted in *The World Treasury of Religious Quotations* (New York: Garland, 1966), 114.

Part 2: Friends

1. Antoine de Saint-Exupéry, *The Little Prince* (Orlando, Fla.: Harcourt, Brace & World, 1943), 66.
2. Maya Angelou, as quoted in *The Rubicon Dictionary of Postive, Motivational, Life-Affirming and Inspirational Quotations,* compiled by John Cook (Newington, Conn.: Rubicon Press, 1993), 95.

3. Helen Keller, *The Quotable Woman* (Philadelphia: Running Press, 1991), 87.
4. Christina Rossetti, *Friendship Is Forever* (New York: Avenel Gramercy-Random House, 1992).
5. John Vianney, as quoted in Jill Adels, *The Wisdom of the Saints* (New York: Oxford University Press, 1987), 16.

Part 3: Homefront

1. Gabrielle Bossis, *He and I* (Sherbrooke, P.Q., Canada: Editions Paulines, 1980), 85.
2. Edward Hays, *Pray All Ways* (Easton, Kansas: Forest of Peace Books, 1981), 11.
3. Heschel, 57.
4. Thomas Merton, *A Seven Day Journey With Thomas Merton* (Ann Arbor, Mich.: Servant, 1992), 40.
5. Thorton Wilder, *Our Town* (New York: Coward-McCann, 1938) (in renewal), Thorton Wilder, 1965, 83.

Part 4: Good-byes

1. Heschel, 65.
2. William Ward, as quoted in Brother Victor-Antoine d'Avila-Latourrette, *This Good Food* (Woodstock, N.Y.: The Overlook Press, 1993), 187.
3. Robert Bellarmine, as quoted in *The Wisdom of the Saints*, 200.
4. Thomas Merton, as quoted in *The Catholic Prayer Book*, compiled by Msgr. Michael Buckley, edited by Tony Castle (Ann Arbor, Mich.: Servant, 1986), 147.
5. T.S. Eliot, as quoted in *The Rubicon Dictionary* 216.

Part 5: Wonder

1. Byrd Baylor Schweitzer, *One Small Blue Bead* (New York: Macmillan, 1965), 11.
2. Katherine Mansfield, as quoted in *The Catholic Prayer Book*, 209.
3. Thomas More, as quoted in *The Catholic Prayer Book*, 97.
4. John Neihardt, *Black Elk Speaks*, (Lincoln, Neb.: University of Nebraska Press, 1961), 1.

5. James Irwin as quoted in *The Home Planet,* edited by Kevin W. Kelley (Reading, Mass.: Addison-Wesley, 1988).
6. P. Fitzgerald, *The New Shorter Oxford English Dictionary* (New York: Oxford University Press, 1993), 3711.
7. Sue Bender, *Plain and Simple* (San Francisco: Harper-San Francisco, 1989), 144.
8. Johannes Kepler, as quoted in the PBS special *Creation of the Universe.*

Part 6: Waiting

1. Elisabeth Elliot, *The Rubicon Dictionary,* 68.
2. Brother Lawrence, *The Practice of the Presence of God,* translated from the French by Robert J. Edmonson (Oleans, Mass.: Paraclete, 1985), 89.

Part 7: On the Road

1. Sr. Mary Paul, *The Rubicon Dictionary,* 179.
2. Ralph L. Woods, editor, *Book of Common Prayer, Third Treasury of the Familiar,* (New York: Macmillan, 1970), 350.
3. Caesarius of Arles, as quoted in *The Wisdom of the Saints,* 15.

Part 8: Nature

1. Thomas Merton, *New Seeds of Contemplation* (New York: New Directions, 1972), 29.
2. Margaret of Cortona, as quoted in *The Wisdom of the Saints,* 186.
3. Old Eskimo saying as quoted in *The Rubicon Dictionary,* 194.
4. Fr. Joseph F. Girzone, *Never Alone* (New York: Doubleday, 1994), 39.

Part 9: Modern Sacramentals

1. Antoine de Saint-Exupéry, 70.
2. James Gleick, *Chaos: Making a New Science* (New York: Viking, 1987), 8.
3. Mother Teresa, *Seeking the Heart of God* (New York: HarperCollins, 1991), 84.